D0292341

formatio
TRADITION. EXPERIENCE.
TRANSFORMATION.

Formatio books from InterVarsity Press follow the rich tradition of the church in the journey of spiritual formation.
These books are not merely about being informed, but about
being transformed by Christ and conformed to his image.
Formatio stands in InterVarsity Press's evangelical publishing
tradition by integrating God's Word with spiritual practice
and by prompting readers to move from inward change to
outward witness. InterVarsity Press uses the chambered nau-
tilus for Formatio, a symbol of spiritual formation because of
its continual spiral journey outward as it moves from its center. We believe that each of us is made with a deep desire to
be in God's presence. Formatio books help us to fulfill our
deepest desires and to become our true selves in light of
God's grace.

RUTH HALEY BARTON

SACRED RHYTHMS

Arranging Our Lives for

Spiritual Transformation

IVP Books

An imprint of InterVarsity Press
Downers Grove, Illinois

InterVarsity Press
P.O. Box 1400, Downers Grove, IL 60515-1426
World Wide Web: www.ivpress.com
E-mail: email@ivpress.com

©2006 by Ruth Haley Barton

All rights reserved. No part of this book may be reproduced in any form without written permission from InterVarsity Press.

InterVarsity Press® is the book-publishing division of InterVarsity Christian Fellowship/USA®, a movement of students and faculty active on campus at hundreds of universities, colleges and schools of nursing in the United States of America, and a member movement of the International Fellowship of Evangelical Students. For information about local and regional activities, write Public Relations Dept., InterVarsity Christian Fellowship/USA, 6400 Schroeder Rd., P.O. Box 7895, Madison, WI 53707-7895, or visit the IVCF website at <www.intervarsity.org>.

Scripture quotations, unless otherwise noted, are from the New Revised Standard Version of the Bible, copyright 1989 by the Division of Christian Education of the National Council of the Churches of Christ in the USA. Used by permission. All rights reserved.

Every effort has been made to contact copyright holders for materials quoted in this book. The author will be pleased to rectify any omissions in future editions if notified by copyright holders.

Design: Cindy Kiple
Images: druvo/iStockphoto

ISBN 978-0-8308-3333-7

Printed in the United States of America ∞

 InterVarsity Press is committed to protecting the environment and to the responsible use of natural resources. As a member of the Green Press Initiative we use recycled paper whenever possible. To learn more about the Green Press Initiative, visit <www.greenpressinitiative.org>.

Library of Congress Cataloging-in-Publication Data

Barton, R. Ruth, 1960-
    Sacred rhythms : arranging our lives for spiritual transformation /
    Ruth Haley Barton.
        p. cm.
    Includes bibliographical references (p.   ).
    ISBN 0-8308-3333-1 (cloth : alk. paper)
    1. Spiritual life—Christianity. I. Title
    BV4501.3.B385 2006
    248.4—dc22

                                                                    2005028345

P   28   27   26   25   24   23   22   21   20   19   18   17   16
Y   25   24   23   22   21   20   19   18   17   16   15   14   13

To the communities of the Transforming Center
with love and gratitude
for your companionship on the journey.
Our shared seeking has called this book forth.

CONTENTS

Introduction

One can begin one's [spiritual] quest by attending to the desires of the heart, both personal and communal. The Spirit is revealed in our genuine hopes for ourselves and for the world. How brightly burns the flame of desire for a love affair with God, other people, the world? Do we know that to desire and seek God is a choice that is always available to us?

ELIZABETH DREYER

Years ago, I sat in a staff meeting at a church I was serving; the purpose of the meeting was to talk about how we could attract more people to join the church. At one point someone counted the requirements for church membership that were already in place and made the startling discovery that somewhere between five and nine time commitments *per week* were required of those who wanted to become church members!

Outwardly I tried to be supportive of the purpose for the meeting, but on the inside I was screaming, *Who would want to sign up for this?* I was already becoming aware of CFS (Christian fatigue syndrome) in my own life and couldn't imagine willingly inflicting it on someone else.

The clarity that dawned in this moment caused me to start being a little more honest about what my own Christian life had been reduced to. While I was trying harder and doing more, there was a yawning emptiness underneath it all that no amount of activity, Christian or otherwise, could fill. It made no difference at all that I had been a Christian all of my conscious life, that I had been in vocational Christian ministry since early adulthood or that I was busy responding to what appeared to be God-given opportunities to become involved in many worthy causes. The more I refused to acknowledge the longing for more, the deeper and wider the emptiness became—until it threatened to swallow me up. In the midst of such barrenness, it was hard to even imagine what Jesus might have meant when he said, "I came that they might have life, and have it abundantly" (John 10:10). My responses to sermons and devotional reflections on this verse were cynical at best. The Christian life just didn't feel that way to me.

It was hard to know where to go to talk about such uncomfortable realities. Life in and around the Christian community does little to help us attend to our longings, to believe that deep within there is something essential that needs to be listened to, or to offer much hope that our deepest longings could take us somewhere good. At times the deeper longings of our heart are dismissed as mere idealism—beyond the realm of possibility this side of heaven. At other times, subtle fear or outright discomfort arises in the face of such expressions of our humanity. The emphasis on human depravity in many religious circles makes it hard to know if there is anything in us that can be trusted.

Sometimes the language of longing is used to stir the emotions of a crowd, but most often what is offered in response is found wanting in the end. Our longing for love is met with relationships that are fairly utilitarian and prone to fall apart under pressure. Our longing for healing and transformation is met with self-help messages that leave us briefly inspired and yet burdened by the pressure of trying to fix ourselves with some new technique or skill. Our longing for a way of life that works is most often met with an invitation to more activity, which unfortunately plays right into our compulsions and the drivenness of Western culture.

My first response to this awareness of longing was to try tweaking my schedule, learning how to say no more decisively, adopting new time management tools. But there comes a time when desire is so deep that mere tweaking is not enough. Finally I just gave in to it all, making the choice to radically reorder my life to listen to the longings of my heart and arrange my life for spiritual seeking. This was a time of utter openness, of questioning almost everything, of letting many of the outward trappings of my life—particularly my spiritual life—fall away until the deepest longings, those that are embedded in the very essence of our humanity, began to be revealed in all of their raw beauty and power. The longing for significance, the longing for love, the longing for deep and fundamental change, the longing for a way of life that *works,* the longing to connect experientially and even viscerally with Someone beyond ourselves—these longings led me to search out spiritual practices and establish life rhythms that promised something more.

⚛ OPENING TO THE MYSTERY OF SPIRITUAL TRANSFORMATION

Perhaps one of the most basic things we need to understand about spiritual transformation is that it is full of mystery. We can be open to it, but we can't accomplish it for ourselves. Paul alludes to this in his writings by using two metaphors. The first is the process by which an embryo is formed in its mother's womb: "I am in labor until Christ be formed in you" (Galatians 4:19). The miracle of conception, the formation of the embryo and the birth process itself are natural but also full of mystery. Even though I have conceived and given birth to three children, even though I have marveled at photos of an embryo forming in its mother's womb, even though I think I understand the facts of life, something in the whole process remains a mystery to me, something I cannot control or make happen. The miracle of birth is always a miracle. It is a God thing. Every single time.

It is the same with the process of metamorphosis. Paul refers to this process in Romans 12:2 when he says, "Do not be conformed to this world but be transformed *[metamorphoō]* by the renewing of your mind."

The Greek word *metamorphoō* is "metamorphosis" in English: the process by which a caterpillar enters into the darkness of the cocoon in order to emerge, eventually, changed almost beyond recognition. This change is so profound that the caterpillar transcends its previous existence to take on a completely different form with a completely different set of capacities. I doubt that the caterpillar has much cognitive understanding of the process itself or the end product. Something much more primal is at work. Something in the very essence of this little being says, *It is time.* And so the caterpillar obeys this inexplicable inner urging and enters in.

Both of these metaphors place the process of spiritual transformation squarely in the category that we call mystery: something outside the range of normal human activity and understanding that can be grasped only through divine revelation and brought about by divine activity.

What does this mean for those of us who are seeking to give ourselves more fully and concretely to the process of spiritual transformation? One thing it means is that whatever we think we might know about it, the decision to give ourselves to the *experience* of spiritual transformation brings us to the very edge of what we know and leaves us peering into the unknown. Even though it is normal for each and every redeemed person to experience spiritual transformation, something about it will always remain a mystery to us. It is one thing to be able to tweak and control external behaviors; it is another thing to experience those internal seismic shifts that change the way I exist in this world—from a worm crawling on my belly to a butterfly winging its way to the sky. *That* kind of change is something only God can do.

In the end, this is the most hopeful thing any of us can say about spiritual transformation: *I cannot transform myself,* or anyone else for that matter. What I can do is create the conditions in which spiritual transformation can take place, by developing and maintaining a rhythm of spiritual practices that keep me open and available to God.

❧ A Journey of Discovery

When we are in touch with our deepest longings (instead of being completely distracted by their surface manifestations), a whole different set of choices opens up. Rather than being motivated by guilt and obligation—as in "I really *ought* to have a quiet time" or "I really *should* pray more"—we are compelled to seek out ways of living that are congruent with our deepest desires. Sometimes this feels risky, and it often opens up a whole new set of questions, but this is fundamentally what spiritual transformation is all about: choosing a way of life that opens us to the presence of God in the places of our being where our truest desires and deepest longings stir. These discoveries are available to all of us as we become more honest in naming what isn't working so that we can craft a way of life that is more congruent with our deepest desires.

The journey begins as we learn to pay attention to our desire in God's presence, allowing our desire to become the impetus for deepening our spiritual journey. This is the substance of the first chapter, and it is not to be taken lightly or skimmed over as a precursor to the disciplines themselves. If we skip this part of the process, our work with the disciplines will be nothing more than another program entered into on the basis of external prodding or superficial motivators. Stay with this chapter for as long as it takes for you to land on something solid within yourself, to discover what it is that you really want. It is not until after we have settled into our desires and named them in God's presence that we are ready to be guided into the spiritual practices that will open us to receive what our heart is longing for.

The movement from desire to discipline is important:

What shapes our actions is basically what shapes our desire. Desire makes us act and when we act what we do will either lead to a greater integration or disintegration within our personalities, minds and bodies—and to the strengthening or deterioration of our relationship to God, others and the world. The habits and disciplines we use to shape our desire form the basis for a spirituality.

Each chapter that follows provides practical guidance for entering into the central disciplines of the Christian faith in such a way that they are linked to the most consistent and compelling desires of the human soul. At the end of every chapter is a practice section that offers you concrete guidance for experiencing each discipline so that you can begin to incorporate them into your everyday life. If you are one who can't help reading a book all the way through, go ahead and do that; however, the greatest benefit will come when you read back through it slowly and actually practice each discipline for as long as it takes for you to feel comfortable with it and experience it a natural expression of your intimacy with God.

This book is not, nor could one book ever be, an exhaustive treatment of all the spiritual disciplines spiritual seekers have used throughout human history. The disciplines explored here are simply the ones that are most basic and needful as a way to begin—like learning the basic steps of a dance or the basic melody of a song. After we explore these basic movements in our relationship with God, chapter nine offers the opportunity to begin putting them together in a patterned way so that we move beyond random, haphazard approaches to the spiritual life. In Christian tradition, this structured arrangement of spiritual practices is referred to as "a rule of life." A rule of life is a way of ordering our life around the values, practices and relationships that keep us open and available to God for the work of spiritual transformation that only God can bring about. Simply put, a rule of life provides structure and space for our growing.

The phrase "spiritual rhythms" is another helpful way of talking about this important concept, because it provides relief from some of the heavy-handed and rigid approaches to the spiritual life that many have experienced. This language draws on the imagery of the natural rhythms of the created order: The ebb and flow of the ocean waves and tides, which come and go steadily but are full of infinite variety and creativity. The predictability of the changing seasons but also the beauty and variance that captures us anew each and every time. The rhythm of a good beat, which makes music and dancing one of the most delightful and spontaneous experiences that we enjoy, yet mastery of the basic notes and moves is required if we are to enter into it fully.

The disciplines themselves are basic components of the rhythm of intimacy with God that feed and nourish the soul, keeping us open and available for God's surprising initiatives in our lives. After we learn the disciplines, there is infinite creativity for putting them together in a rhythm that works for us and great freedom for adding other disciplines and creative elements.

The caterpillar must yield up the life it knows and submit to the mystery of interior transformation. It emerges from the process transfigured, with wings that give it freedom to fly. . . . A rule of life gives us a way to enter into the life-long process of personal transformation. Its disciplines help us to shed the familiar but constricting "old self" and allow our "new self" in Christ to be formed—the true self that is naturally attracted to the light of God.

MARJORIE THOMPSON,
SOULFEAST

✲ AN INVITATION TO COMMUNITY

Although this book's emphasis is on personal spiritual disciplines, the spiritual journey was never meant to be taken alone. The whole of Scripture bears this out, but Jesus' life in particular offers us a compelling example. At the very beginning of Jesus' ministry, after praying and listening to God all night, he chose a small community of twelve disciples—"those whom he wanted," the Scriptures tell us. He chose them first "to be with him" (Mark 3:13-14) and then to do the work of ministry. Jesus' first invitation was for them to be together with him in community, shaped by his teaching and leadership, and he remained faithful to these relationships until the end of his life.

Our commitment to community and to spiritual friendship within that community is in itself a spiritual discipline that is of great significance to the spiritual life. Spiritual friendship is not primarily a social relationship that exists for the purpose of catching up over lunch or an occasional lunch or a golf outing. It is not primarily a collegial relationship focused on work matters or service projects. It is not a self-help relationship focused primarily on problem solving or accountability. It is not even primarily a Bible study group. Rather it is a relationship that is focused intentionally on our relationship with God as viewed through the lens of desire. With such a friend we share the deepest desires of our heart, so that we can support one another in arranging our lives in ways that are congruent with what our hearts want most. Together we reverence the ways God is meeting us in the context of the spiritual practices that help us to seek him.

Community is such a crucial element of the formation process that it will be addressed as a theme woven throughout the book. Furthermore, you are also invited to *experience* community by choosing a friend or two or even a small group with whom to take the journey, using the guidance provided in the "Journeying Together" appendix. This appendix will guide you in experiencing each discipline together and will also provide questions to help you debrief your experience. Thus the spiritual disciplines form the basis for your interactions with others in community, and your life in community becomes a safe place to practice the patterns and behaviors that bring about substantive change. If you have friends who seem to share a capacity and a desire to enter more deeply into the spiritual journey, invite them to join you so that none of you have to take the journey alone.

✺

There are moments in our lives when we cry out inwardly, *I don't care what anyone else says; there has to be more to the Christian life than this!* This book is for those moments in your life and mine. It is about hearing Jesus speak right into such moments with whispers of understanding and hope: "There are desires in you that are so deep and so true and so connected to the essence of who you are; those are the desires I want to meet—and not just partially, but abundantly."

May Jesus Christ himself meet us in the place of our spiritual seeking.

1

LONGING FOR MORE

An Invitation to Spiritual Transformation

The reason we are not able to see God is the faintness of our desire.

MEISTER ECKHART

One of the things that still surprises me this far along in life is how and when and with what power my longing stirs. Certain times are fairly predictable—times when I am tired from travel and missing home and family, seasons when I have been overly busy and long to be with God for God's own sake, certain moments in the holiday season when I hunger for a deeper experience of the meaning of things. To some extent I have grown accustomed to these longings and know what to do with them. But there are other times when longing ambushes me with a ferocity that seems all out of proportion to what is going on at the moment; it catches me up short with the awareness that something here warrants my attention. Although the experience of longing and desire is often bittersweet, it reminds me that I am alive in ways that I want to be alive.

A few years ago our daughter Bethany was celebrating her fifteenth birthday. It was September of her first year in high school, and all she wanted was to have a party with fifty of her closest friends. (That was *after* she had gone over the guest list with a fine-toothed comb and whittled it down from seventy-five!) While it was a little daunting to think about hosting the first party of the year for fifty new high-schoolers, it was what she wanted, so our whole family rallied to the occasion. Bethany's older sister, Charity (who was a senior at the time) corralled some of her friends to organize and do the judging for a karaoke competition. Very cool. I fixed and served the food. My husband, Chris, patrolled the premises to make sure visitors carrying unwanted substances didn't find their way to the party. Younger sister Haley just tried to stay out of the way.

At one point in the evening, I became alert to the fact that something important was going on, something that was connected with the deepest longings of my heart. As kids were going through the food line and fixing their hamburgers and hot dogs, they were all very polite, but there was one young man whose expression of appreciation was so genuine that I stopped what I was doing and paid attention. He said, "Thanks for letting us do this, Mrs. Barton. This is so much fun!"

I looked up from serving, met his eyes and said, "You're welcome. We really enjoy having you!"

He paused mid-ketchup, returned my gaze and said with incredulity, "Really?" as though he was completely unaccustomed to being enjoyed.

The young man's unguarded response combined disbelief and wonderment so sweetly that I was flooded with awareness and suddenly saw my life in a way I had never seen it before. Something inside me stood at attention and said, *This is my life. This is what it's like to be all the way here now rather than always longing for something else. This is my life as it is meant to be lived in God.*

That moment passed as quickly as it came, one of many that made it a delightful evening. Our whole family had banded together to do something special for one of us, and it felt good. When it was all over, we collapsed in our family room, utterly exhausted, and reflected on the evening. We laughed about the karaoke contest and commented on who could sing and who couldn't. We took a leisurely look at the gifts Bethany had received. We talked about what a good time everyone seemed to have and how polite and appreciative they had been. And the thought came anew: *This is my best self. This is who I want to be more and more, by God's grace. These are the moments I will remember on my deathbed and say, "That was what I was meant for."*

Then it ambushed me—my longing, that is. A prayer welled up from the depths of my being, a prayer so full of desire that it was barely articulate: "O God, give me more moments like this—moments when I am fully present to you and to others in love. Moments when I am connected with what is purest and most authentic within me and able to respond to your presence in that place. I want to live my life in such a way that there is more of this!"

There are other moments, as well, when longing stirs. There was the perilous summer when I turned forty. As the actual birthday approached and the party was being planned, I realized that I did not want a party where people stood around holding a drink and making small talk. This time it was the longing for love that took me by surprise. When I really listened, I realized that what I most wanted was to give and receive love—really—on that day. I wanted to be with friends and family. I wanted to have time. I wanted to share from the heart and know that we had seen each other and heard each other and put into words how much we mattered to each other. How surprising to notice that underneath the noise and activity of my "adult" life, such simple and tender longings stirred.

And so that's what we did. We canceled the party, and instead I had opportunities to spend time individually with those most precious to me throughout the day: breakfast, lunch, dinner and everything in between! What a wonderful day it was—a day full of love given and received.

Then there are the times when I am aware of my brokenness, and a longing for real, fundamental change groans within me. In one season of my life I experienced a betrayal so deep that for quite some time I was almost paralyzed in relating to anyone outside of my most intimate circle of family and friends. While I had the normal feelings of anger and outrage, sadness and grief, there was an even deeper longing—the longing to be healed. I was aware that I had turned inward, had closed my heart. Distrust and suspicion had made me hard-edged and withdrawn, and I found myself crying out to God to do something within me that I could not do for myself. Something that would enable me, once again, to be given over to God and to others with the kind of trust and abandon I had known before the betrayal.

Regardless of the pain I had experienced, I did not want to live forever in a hardened and broken state. For the first time, the Jesus Prayer— uttered by the blind and the broken in Christ's day—began to pray itself in me unbidden: *Lord Jesus Christ, have mercy on me, a sinner.* I knew that whatever needed to be done in me, God would have to do, for I was incapable of fixing myself.

✖ NAMING OUR DESIRE IN CHRIST'S PRESENCE

When was the last time you felt it—your own longing, that is? Your longing for love, your longing for God, your longing to live *your* life as it is meant to be lived in God? When was the last time you felt a longing for healing and fundamental change groaning within you?

Do not rush past this question; it may be the most important question you ever ask. But this is hard, I know. In religious circles we are much more accustomed to silencing our desire, distancing ourselves from it, because we are suspicious and afraid of its power. *Isn't there something better I should be doing with my time?* we ask ourselves. *Something a little less dangerous and unpredictable? Something more selfless and spiritual?* And besides, desire is such a volatile thing. Are not my desires shot through with human deception and sinful urges? What if they overtake me and propel me down a path I ought not travel? Worse yet, what if I touch that place of longing and desire within me and let myself really feel how deep it goes, only to discover that those desires cannot be met? What will I do with myself then? How will I live with desire that is awake and alive rather than asleep and repressed?

These are some of the deepest questions of the human soul, and they defy any attempt at simplistic answers. In the midst of my own discomfort with such penetrating questions, I have found it surprising but also reassuring to enter into the biblical story and discover that Jesus himself routinely asked people questions that helped them to get in touch with their desire and name it in his presence. He often brought focus and clarity to his interactions with those who were spiritually hungry by asking them, "What do you want? What do you want me to do for you?" Such questions had the power to elicit deeply honest reflection in the person to whom they were addressed, and opened the way for Christ to lead them into deeper levels of spiritual truth and healing.

In the story of Jesus' encounter with blind Bartimaeus on the Jericho road, for instance, the question about desire is the pivot point. We don't know how long Bartimaeus had been spending his days begging by the side of the road, but on this particular day Bartimaeus heard that Jesus was passing by, and he had a sense of new spiritual possibility. Perhaps Jesus could do something for him that no one else had been able to do. Perhaps Jesus could do what he had been hoping for and dreaming of for so long.

But it was noisy and crowded in the city that day, and it would be hard to get anyone's attention, let alone someone as busy and important as this popular young teacher, who was always, it seemed, surrounded by disciples and questioners. In order to get Jesus' attention above the din of the crowd, Bartimaeus had to reach deep within, touch that place of fundamental human need and desire, and cry out from that place. "Jesus, Son of David, have mercy on me!"

And Jesus heard him that day, above all the other voices that were clamoring for his attention. The honesty, the desperation, the humanness of the cry was completely arresting. The people around him were embarrassed by such an honest expression of need and tried to silence him, but Bartimaeus's soul cry so captured Jesus' attention that it stopped him in his tracks. He stood still in the middle of the road and summoned Bartimaeus to himself. As they stood face to face, Jesus asked the question that required Bartimaeus to name his desire: "What do you want me to do for you?"

Now if I had been in Bartimaeus's shoes, I might have gotten a little impatient with a question whose answer was so obvious. "What do you mean, 'What do you want me to do for you?' Isn't it obvious? And besides, this is getting a little personal, don't you think? We don't know each other *that* well!"

But on another level, the level where the spiritual journey is unfolding, it is a question that penetrates to the very core of our being. And it *is* very, very personal. It brings us face to face with our humanness, our vulnerability, our need. If we let it, such a question strips away the layers of pretense and superficiality to expose what is truest within us. And that is a very tender place indeed.

Your desire for more of God than you have right now, your longing for love, your need for deeper levels of spiritual transformation than you have experienced so far is the truest thing about you. You might think that your woundedness or your sinfulness is the truest thing about you or that your giftedness or your personality type or your job title or your identity as husband or wife, mother or father, somehow defines you. But in reality, it is your desire for God and your capacity to reach for more of God than you have right now that is the deepest essence of who you are. There is a place within each one of us that is spiritual in nature, the place where God's Spirit witnesses with our spirit about our truest identity. Here God's Spirit dwells with our spirit, and here our truest desires make themselves known. From this place we cry out to God for deeper union with him and with others.

❧ DESIRE AS THE BEGINNING OF THE SPIRITUAL JOURNEY

When we pay attention to our longing and allow questions about our longing to strip away the outer layers of self-definition, we are tapping into the deepest dynamic of the spiritual life. The stirring of spiritual desire indicates that God's Spirit is already at work within us, drawing us to himself. We love God because he first loved us. We long for God because he first longed for us. We reach for God because he first reached for us. Nothing in the spiritual life originates with us. It all originates with God.

So it is that the spiritual life begins in this most unlikely place. It begins with the longing that stirs way down deep, underneath the noise, the activity, the drivenness of our life. But it is not always comfortable to acknowledge such longing, and the direction that such an admission takes us is different for all of us.

When James and John (and later on their mother) answered Jesus' question about desire by asking that they be granted positions of prominence in Jesus' kingdom—one on his right and one on his left—it exposed false ambition that was detrimental to them and to the community of disciples. Similarly, there are desires within us that work against the life of the Spirit within us—desires rooted in selfish ambition, pride, lust, fear, self-protection and many other unexamined motives. These desires lurk within all of us, and that is why giving any attention at all to desire feels like opening up Pandora's box. But it is even riskier to refuse to acknowledge what's real within us, because whether we acknowledge them or not, these dynamics are at work wielding a subterranean power over us. Their power only gets stronger the longer we repress them. How much safer it is for ourselves and everyone around us if we open up our desires in Jesus' presence and allow him to help us sift through them.

As disturbing as it is to be exposed in this way, sometimes it is exactly what we need. For then Jesus can gently strip away that which is false and destructive in our desire and fan into flames those desires that are good and true.

Listening to Jesus' response to James and John, you can almost feel his compassion and love for them. "You do not know what you are asking. Are you able to drink the cup that I am about to drink?" (Matthew 20:23). The disciples' ability to be this honest with Jesus about the deeper dynamics stirring within them was a new kind of intimacy that opened the way for him to begin the process of making right that which was not right within them. One can only hope that such a penetrating comment and question served to begin releasing these disciples from desires that were not their truest ones. If they had not been honest with Jesus about what was going on inside, their darker desires would have functioned underground and probably have eventually destroyed their relationships with the other disciples and their ministry.

Opening up our desire in God's presence—even when we're not sure which parts are true and which are false—is humbling, but it gives God a chance to help us sort it all out. There is another possibility as well. Sometimes when we open up our desire in Christ's presence, we find ourselves needing to discern what is our part and what is God's part in this process of living into our heart's deepest desire. When Jesus met the paralyzed man at the Pool of Bethesda, his question about desire was even more pointed. "Do you want to be made well?" he asked (John 5:6). In other words, How bad do you want it? Do you want it bad enough to do something about it?

How Bad Do You Want It?

I have spent a lot of time on the sidelines of youth soccer games and have witnessed all sorts of obnoxiousness on the part of soccer parents. But every so often a bit of truth presents itself in this unlikeliest of places. One day a particularly overbearing father was yelling at two fourth-grade girls who were converging on the ball and trying to win it for their team. In an attempt to be motivating, he screamed (among other things), "How bad do you want it? You've got to really want it!"

Though I was annoyed by such a display of unbridled emotion by an adult at a children's game, I was struck by the truth contained in his statement. The depth of desire has a great deal to do with the outcome of our life. Often, those who accomplish what they set out to do in life are not those who are the most talented or gifted or who have had the best opportunities. Often they are the ones who are most deeply in touch with how badly they want whatever they want; they are the ones who consistently refuse to be deterred by the things that many of us allow to become excuses.

The paralytic was full of excuses: "I have no one to put me into the pool when the water is stirred up; and while I am making my way, someone else steps down ahead of me." Jesus' response, in effect, was "Never mind all that. Stand up, take up your mat and walk" (John 5:6-9). Then the paralyzed man reached within himself to that place of deep desire and deep faith and did what he was told. And somehow his willingness to follow his desire opened the way for him to experience Jesus' healing power.

> *The more authentic our desires, the more they touch upon our identities and also upon the reality of God at the heart of our being. Our most authentic desires spring ultimately from the deep inner wells where the longing for God runs freely.*
>
> PHILLIP SHELDRAKE,
> *BEFRIENDING OUR DESIRES*

Jesus' interactions with the people he came in contact with during his life on earth make it clear that desire, and the willingness to name that desire in Christ's presence, is a catalytic element of the spiritual life. It is one of the most powerful motivators for a life lived consistently with intentionality and focus. Beyond that, the willingness to open up this tender and sometimes volatile place in Christ's presence is part of the intimacy we seek. Somehow it creates the possibility for Christ to be with us in a way that meets our truest need. It enables us to rise up from our place by the side of the road so that we can actually get on the path to spiritual transformation and follow Christ.

❧ PRACTICE

Settle into a comfortable position that allows you to remain alert. Breathe deeply in this moment as a way of releasing any tension you might be holding and becoming aware of God's presence, which is closer than your breath. Allow yourself to enjoy God's presence in quietness for a few moments.

When you feel ready, imagine yourself in the historical setting of the story of Bartimaeus as it unfolds in Mark 10:46-52, or imagine yourself in your own place of need. Read the story slowly, seeing yourself as the person needing something from Christ and calling out to him from the noisy crowd. How do you approach him or try to get his attention? What words do you use? What emotions do you feel?

Imagine that in response to your cry, Jesus turns to you. Now you are face to face with one another. Allow yourself the full realization that you have Jesus' complete attention (because you do!) and hear his question addressed to you: "What do you want me to do for you?"

Do not be afraid of emotion; it is important that you let yourself feel how deep your desire goes. You may need to sit with the question and your response for quite some time before you have fully gotten in touch with your heart's desire or have fully expressed it. Give this question and its answer all the time it needs. You may want to go for a walk with the question, lie in the grass and feel the warmth of the sun, curl up under a blanket, journal your response, engage in writing or artistic expression.

If you choose to journal, it might help to begin with the statement "God, what I most need/want from you right now is . . ." and then let your thoughts flow. Listen for Christ's response.

Don't feel as if you have to do anything; simply relish the intimacy and richness that come when we are able to "be with what is" in God's presence.

2

SOLITUDE

Creating Space for God

*The soul is like a wild animal—tough, resilient, resourceful, savvy,
self-sufficient. It knows how to survive in hard places. But it is also
shy. Just like a wild animal, it seeks safety in the dense underbrush.
If we want to see a wild animal, we know that the last thing we should
do is go crashing through the woods yelling for it to come out.
But if we will walk quietly into the woods, sit patiently by the base of
the tree, and fade into our surroundings, the wild animal we seek
might put in an appearance.*

PARKER PALMER, *A HIDDEN WHOLENESS*

I will never forget my first experience with extended solitude. It was a
field trip, of sorts, that was part of a seminary class on spiritual formation
in which we were exploring different elements of the spiritual life. As a
conclusion to the class, we went on retreat together in order to experience an extended time in solitude. While I had been practicing shorter
times of solitude in the context of normal life, this was the first time anyone had invited me to unplug completely and enter into a whole day of
solitude. Our class had been instructed to gather at a nearby retreat center, where we would spend the day on retreat under the guidance of our
beloved professor.

The morning was wonderful but in some ways very similar to what I had already been experiencing; however, when lunchtime came, something new began to take shape. We were told that we would eat lunch in silence so as not to interrupt our attention to God by being drawn into social interaction. Our host guided us to a beautiful dining room with windows on three sides looking out over the grounds of the retreat center and the woods beyond. A hot lunch had been prepared, and the chairs were set up facing the windows so that each person could look to the outside while we were eating. As we entered the dining room in silence, it was as if something broke open inside of me. I was caught completely off guard. Tears started sneaking down my face, and I stood sniffling with no Kleenex in sight, wondering what in the world was happening to me!

The first feeling I could identify was the sheer relief of knowing that I wouldn't have to talk to anyone or do anything or serve anyone during this lunch. For once, my place with God in solitude was being honored—not managed or directed or interpreted by a pastor or a Bible study leader or anyone else who thought they knew what I needed. For once, I wasn't going to have to force myself into someone else's prefabricated plan for my spiritual enrichment. I was so glad we had been instructed not to talk, because this meant no one could intrude by asking me what was wrong and trying to "help." I needed to be alone with what was happening inside. Because I had space to feel what I was feeling, I could begin acknowledging truth that I had not known how to name before.

All of a sudden I was awake and alert to a level of overstimulation and exhaustion that I had come to associate with normal Christian living. As I let my emotions flow without censoring them or trying to talk myself out of them, I could feel the weight of Christian expectations that I had been carrying around unawares. There were the expectations around being a godly spouse. There was the weight of expectation to be a good parent (my children were eleven, nine and five at the time) and trying to balance that with the demands of my professional life. There was the seriousness with which my husband and I took our responsibilities as church members and as a churchgoing family and all the busyness that went along with that. There was the book I had just finished that had drained me of every last meaningful word I could think of. There were all of my attempts to be a good neighbor, to be a good Christian, to be a good everything.

These had worn me down so completely that here I was, overwhelmed with emotion at the simplest gift—someone fixing me a meal and allowing me the freedom to sit in silence with God while I ate it. Nothing to do. Nothing to say. No social interaction to try to figure out. How, I wondered, had my life in Christ gotten reduced to so much busyness, so many words, such weighty expectations? How had I gotten this far in the spiritual life without anyone ever having told me that it was OK to stop talking and stop doing and just *be* in God's presence? What was I to do with the pent-up longing and frustration that was now expressing itself in these unexpected tears?

For yet another reason it was a good thing we were not allowed to talk to each other: it would have been so easy to run away into conversation or to look someplace outside myself for answers. Instead, I had to snuffle my way through lunch and stay present to God, who was my mealtime companion. I had to stay with my longings in his presence and get honest about the ways my life *as I was living it* was not congruent with my heart's deepest desires. This was a stunning realization; after all, I had made most of my own life choices. How had I ended up here? *Lord have mercy.* What was one to *do* with such longing and depth of feeling?

⧉ SOLITUDE: A PLACE FOR DESIRE

Most of us are not very good at sitting with longing and desire—our own or someone else's. It feels tender. It feels vulnerable. It feels out of control. It is a place where one human being cannot fix or fill another, nor can we fix or fill ourselves. It is a place where only God will do.

The longing for solitude is the longing for God. It is the longing to experience union with God unmediated by the ways we typically try to relate to God. By "unmediated" I mean a direct experience of God with nothing in between: an encounter with God that is not mediated by words, by theological constructs, by religious activity, by my own or other's manipulations of my relationship with God. It is the practice that spiritual seekers down through the ages have used to *experience* intimacy with God rather than just talking about it.

Solitude is a place. It is a place in time that is set apart for God and God alone, a time when we unplug and withdraw from the noise of interpersonal interactions, from the noise, busyness and constant stimulation associated with life in the company of others. Solitude can also be associated with a physical place that has been set apart for times alone with God, a place that is not cluttered with work, noise, technology, other relationships, or any of those things that call us back into doing mode. Most important, solitude is a place inside myself where God's Spirit and my spirit dwell together in union. This place within me is private and reserved for the intimacies that God and I share. What happens between the two of us in that place is not meant for public consumption. It is a place where I can give myself with abandon to the Lover of my soul, knowing that I am completely safe from anyone else's curious gaze or judgmental glance.

Silence deepens our experience of solitude, because in silence we choose to unplug not only from the constant stimulation of life in the company of others but also from our own addiction to noise, words and activity. It creates a space for listening to the knowings that go beyond words, and feeling no pressure at all to put the depths of the human soul into words. We enter into solitude and silence on the basis of our desire for God, and it becomes a place for being with our desire in God's presence. Even if we also experience some resistance (which is quite normal, especially in the beginning), when the desire is deep enough to overcome our resistance, we are on our way. The most essential question in solitude is *How have I been wanting to be with God, and how has God been wanting to be with me?*

⚬ A PLACE FOR THE SOUL TO COME OUT

The longing for solitude is also the longing to find ourselves, to be in touch with what is most real within us, that which is more solid and enduring than what defines us externally. This is our soul, that place at the very center of our being that is known by God, that is grounded in God and is one with God.

But it's tricky to get the soul to come out, as Parker Palmer so eloquently acknowledges. We are not very safe for ourselves, because our internal experience involves continual critique and judgment, and the tender soul does not want to risk it. Unfortunately, a lot of our religious activity is very noisy as well; oftentimes we're just an organized group of people crashing through the woods together, making so much noise that there's not a soul in sight.

There are very few places where the soul is truly safe, where the knowing, the questions, the longings of the soul are welcomed, received and listened to rather than evaluated, judged or beaten out of us. The experience I recounted earlier was a time when my soul "came out" and told me things that it had been impossible to know while I was crashing so noisily through the woods of my life. I imagine my soul crouching under a leafy bush, shaking its head, saying, "I just cannot talk to her when she's like this!" It took a half a day in solitude followed by a silent lunch for me to get anywhere near quiet enough on the inside to know what was really going on. Then when I did figure out what was going on, it took more time in solitude to invite God into that place to help me, rather than allowing others to rush in or allowing myself to rush out.

It reminds me of a story about a priest who observed a woman sitting in the empty church with her head in her hands. An hour passed, then two. She was still there. Judging her to be a soul in distress and eager to be of assistance, at last the priest approached the woman and said, "Is there any way I can be of help?"

"No thank you, Father," she said, "I've been getting all the help I need until you interrupted!"

In solitude we allow God to help us. Thank goodness solitude was the discipline of that day, because it kept all of us from rushing in and interrupting the work of God in each other's lives.

✎ UNPLUGGING AND LISTENING

It is not easy to create this kind of space for attention to the deeper dynamics of the soul in God's presence. There is nothing in Western culture or even in our religious subculture to support us in entering into these times for "unproductive" being rather than frenetic doing. A decade or so ago, when our society was on the cusp of many technological breakthroughs that we now take for granted, there was much editorializing about the hope that we could look forward to four-day work weeks and still get the same amount done. That has not happened. In fact, the drivenness of our pace of life has become even more pronounced; rather than working five nine-to-five days a week, we find that technology has made it more difficult to have any boundaries around our working life. Since we can access voicemail, e-mail and the Internet from anywhere, many of us work six or seven days a week. Technology was supposed to help us lead saner lives, but instead it has led us to expect more of ourselves and try to cram more in.

One of the new challenges for our generation is the impact of technology on our spirituality. This warrants serious consideration. If we are not careful, technology has a way of compromising our ability to be present to ourselves, to God and to each other—all of which are fundamental elements of the spiritual life. I don't know about you, but I am sad when I have set aside time to be with friends and, because a cell phone is left on, we are at the mercy of all manner of intrusion. We think nothing of taking phone calls in the middle of meetings, restaurants and family gatherings. I am disturbed by my own compulsion to check e-mail late at night and first thing in the morning. When left unchecked, this lack of discipline imperceptibly robs me of rest in the evening and silent presence to God in the morning. I can become exhausted by the intrusion of the media and technology into every corner of my life, resulting in constant overstimulation of body, mind and emotions. All of this convenience wears me out!

Exhaustion sets in when we are too accessible too much of the time. A soul-numbing sadness comes when we realize that a certain quality of life and quality of presence is slipping away as a result of too much "convenience." Breaks in the day that used to be small windows of replenishment for body and soul—like driving in a car, going for a walk, having lunch with a friend—are now filled with noise, interruption and multitasking. What feels like being available and accessible is really a boundaryless existence that offers no protection for those things that are most precious to us.

While technology promises that we will be more connected and able to "reach out and touch someone" anytime we want, over time it results in a kind of fragmentation. Recently I was driving through our neighborhood on a spectacular spring day and noticed three people out on walks—one with a child, one walking a dog and one walking alone. The three had one thing in common: they were all on cell phones! It dawned on me that just a few short years ago, this would have been completely impossible: a walk outdoors would be at least one time when we could count on unplugging and being fully present in the moment.

No wonder we feel disconnected from God: we are rarely able to give him our full attention in solitude and silence. Thoughtful reflection is constantly sabotaged by the intrusion of cell phones, pagers and e-mail messages. No wonder our human relationships are so unsatisfying as they get reduced to snippets of interrupted, disembodied phone conversation. What feels like convenience is actually robbing us of those things we value most. We are left with bits and pieces of everything rather than experiencing the full substance of anything.

It's not that I am averse to technology; I too have a cell phone, an office phone, a home phone and an e-mail address, and they are much needed. However, I am aware of longings that run much deeper than what technology can address. I am noticing that the more I fill my life with the convenience of technology, the emptier I become in the places of my deepest longing. I long for the beauty and substance of being in the presence of those I love, even though it is less convenient. I long for spacious, thoughtful conversation even though it is less efficient. I long to be connected with my authentic self, even though it means being inaccessible to others at times. I long to be one who waits and listens deeply for the still, small voice of God, even if it means I must unplug from technology in order to become quiet enough to hear.

Constant noise, interruption and drivenness to be more productive cut us off from or at least interrupt the direct experience of God and other human beings, and this is more isolating than we realize. Because we are experiencing less meaningful human and divine connection, we are emptier relationally, and we try harder and harder to fill that loneliness with even more noise and stimulation. In so doing we lose touch with the quieter and more subtle experiences of God within.

This is a vicious cycle indeed.

Solitude is an opportunity to interrupt this cycle by turning off the noise and stimulation of our lives so that we can hear our loneliness and our longing calling us deeper into the only relationship that can satisfy our longing.

GETTING IN TOUCH WITH WHAT'S TRUE ABOUT US

Just recently I was able to schedule several days in solitude under the guidance of a spiritual director. It had been a long time since I had had any extended time in solitude, and I was spent. Travel and speaking, ministry and retreat leadership, writing deadlines and family responsibilities had snowballed to the point that life had become almost unmanageable, and my soul had paid a price.

As I drove toward the retreat site and allowed myself to begin to settle into God's presence, I was aware of deep unrest at the core of my being. There were private places of pain and disillusionment that I had been trying to shore up with inspirational pep talks that sounded an awful lot like someone else's rhetoric rather than God's word to me. Decisions were weighing on me, but I was so exhausted I didn't trust my own judgment. My ability to love and trust was worn so thin from the wear and tear of life that I feared I was becoming deformed rather than transformed. Spiritual longings were stirring powerfully within me, and I was exhausted from trying to manage such unwieldy forces. As I drove to the place of my retreat, I heard myself asking, "Is there any hope for me?" It was the first time I had ever wondered that about myself.

I wept all the way through my first spiritual direction session. From one topic to another, each one brought a fresh wave of tears. Finally my spiritual director said, "Your soul is tired and battered. You can't do anything until you rest, and it may take longer than you think." Solitude had to be a place of rest for me before it could turn into anything else.

This is the way it is for most of us. Most of us are more tired than we know *at the soul level.* We are teetering on the brink of dangerous exhaustion, and we really cannot do anything else until we have gotten some rest. The other disciplines described in this book and elsewhere are a wonderful smorgasbord of spiritual sustenance, but we really can't engage any of them until solitude becomes a place of rest for us rather than another place for human striving and hard work.

Jesus seemed to be highly attentive to this particular danger of the spiritual life, because early on in his ministry with the disciples, he began to teach them about the importance of unplugging from the demands of life in the company of others for the purpose of resting in God. In Mark 6:30, Jesus invites his disciples to "come away to a deserted place all by yourselves and rest a while." This verse is often lifted out of context, which is fine because it is a simple, powerful imperative. But it is even more compelling when taken in context.

If we go back to the beginning of Mark 6, we discover that Jesus had just commissioned the disciples for ministry and had given them the authority to cast out demons, preach the gospel and heal the sick. These were exciting times, but also times of great spiritual exertion and emotional complexity, for they had experienced a devastating loss: John the Baptist had been beheaded on the silliest of whims, and it had been their job to retrieve the body and bury it. It is hard to imagine the emotional toll of caring for the beheaded body of the one who had proclaimed the way of the Lord with such power and grace.

In the midst of all this—the first flush of ministry success and also the grief of deep personal loss—the disciples crowd around Jesus and report on all they have done and taught. You can almost hear the kinds of things they might have said:

- "You won't believe it! We spoke to a demon that was holding someone in bondage and he left the person!"
- "We preached the gospel and called for people to come forward and repent, and they all came forward!"
- "There was this person who was crippled, and we anointed him with oil and he was cured! It's unbelievable what's happening out there!"

But Jesus seems to have little time for their ministry reports. He is concerned about the bigger issue of how they will sustain their spiritual life rather than being distracted by outward successes. Without wasting any time at all, he invites them to experience solitude as a place of rest in God.

Like us, they are surrounded by people who have needs, and it is no small thing to extricate themselves from the human morass that surrounds them. No sooner have they set their course and gotten into a boat to leave than the crowd sees what they are doing, takes off on foot and arrives ahead of them. The "deserted place" that Jesus was leading them to is no longer very solitary!

Yet Jesus remains undeterred. He has compassion on the crowd because he sees how spiritually lost they are, and he does lead the disciples in meeting the people's needs. He multiplies the meager five loaves and two fishes into a meal for five thousand men plus women and children—and in the process he also multiplies the disciples' meager energies so that they can stay present and help. But before the miracle is even cleaned up, Jesus is back on mission and says to them, "I'll finish up here. You go on ahead to that solitary place, because that is still what you need most" (see Mark 6:45). What is behind Jesus' single-minded focus and intentionality around leading his disciples to a place of rest?

❧ LEARNING TO REST IN GOD

Jesus knows how quickly our passions, even the most noble, can wear us out if we're not careful. I think he also understands that the sources of our exhaustion are many and complex and often we are completely unaware of how they are taking their toll. There are the obvious sources of exhaustion like a heavy workload, many family responsibilities, busy seasons when extra activity crowds in, but there are more subtle sources of inner exhaustion as well. We might be functioning out of an inordinate sense of "ought and should," burdened by unrealistic expectations about what it means to be a good Christian. Since we're not always sure how to live with our humanness, we feel guilty when we are tired, ill or grieving and try to shove it down rather than attend to it. But it takes energy to repress these aspects of our humanness, and eventually the effort itself wears us out.

We might have few or no boundaries on our work or availability to others and be driven by the feeling that we should be doing more because there is always more to do. While our nonstop pace may be tied to genuine passion for what we do (as it was in the disciples' case), we can reach a point where our genuine gifts and passions wear us out because we don't know when to stop.

There are darker possibilities as well. It could be that we are driven by a need to perform and feel that we are worthwhile only when we are achieving and doing. We find it hard to enter into solitude because it threatens our sense of who we are. Or unresolved tension and toxicity in some relationships may be very draining, but we don't feel free to extricate ourselves from them. Thus we are carrying a great burden of unhealed wounds thinking that we should be able to handle it ,when in reality it is draining our life energy day by day.

When deeper levels of exhaustion set in, there is a slippage in our spiritual practices, because we do start to feel that we are beyond hope and we don't have energy even for the disciplines and rhythms that are normally life giving for us. Over time, we fail to receive the natural replenishment that flows from a rhythm of meaningful spiritual practices, and we suffer inner drought.

Jesus seeks to guide his disciples—then and now—into rhythms of solitude, community and ministry. In such a rhythm, solitude helps us stay attentive to the dynamics of spiritual exhaustion and attend to the deeper sources before they pull us under. One of the most important lessons I have learned over the past few years is how important it is to have time and space for being with what's real in my life—to celebrate the joys, grieve the losses, shed my tears, sit with the questions, feel my anger, attend to my loneliness. This "being with what is" is not the same thing as problem solving or fixing, because not everything can be fixed or solved. Rather, it means allowing God to be with me in that place and waiting for him to do what is needed. *In silence my soul waits for you and you alone, O God. From you alone comes my salvation.*

When we don't attend to our vulnerabilities and instead try to repress it all and keep soldiering on, we get weary from holding it in. Eventually it leaks out in ways that are damaging to us and to others.

Another reason we are so tired is that we are always working hard to figure things out rather than learning how to cease striving, how to be with what is true *in God's presence* and let God be God in the most intimate places of our life—which is, in the end, the only thing that will change anything. We're busy trying to make stuff happen rather than waiting on God to make stuff happen.

There are many Scripture texts that speak to the importance of waiting for God's action and initiative; one of my favorites is a little verse in Exodus 14. The Israelites are literally backed into a corner: the Red Sea is in front of them and the Egyptians are gaining on them from behind, intent on taking them back into captivity or destroying them. They are already complaining to Moses about the miserable failure their escape plan has turned out to be. Moses responds firmly, "Do not be afraid, stand firm, and see the deliverance that the Lord will accomplish for you today; for the Egyptians whom you see today you shall never see again. [And here is my favorite part.] *The Lord will fight for you, and you have only to keep still*" (Exodus 14:13-14).

One of the fundamental purposes of solitude is to give us a concrete way of entering into such stillness, so that God can come in and do what only God can do. For the most part, I'm not sure we human beings are capable of being still and letting God fight for us without a discipline to help us do it. This is a very deep kind of rest indeed.

❧ What I Know for Sure

Not long ago, I wrote a book that chronicled my own journey into solitude and silence over the last fifteen years. The challenge of writing this chapter has been to do so without relying too much on what I have written before.

It seems God has used this as an opportunity to push me to look deep into my current experience with solitude and has asked, "What do you know about it now? What can you say *now* that represents the truth of your current experience with this most significant Christian discipline?"

What has come to me in response to God's question is so startling that to write it feels almost like True Confessions, but here it is: *The only time when I am not lonely and my longing for union is satisfied is when I am in solitude.* In the world of people and things, I do sometimes experience moments that have a sense of completeness—moments of union with God and others and the world beyond—but most times these moments are fleeting and give only a taste of what my heart is longing for. The truth is, they often seem to exacerbate longings that I now know will never be completely satisfied here on this earth. No matter how beautiful such moments are, they are often fraught with a painful awareness of human separateness even from those we love the most, and I am left trying to manage my unruly tendencies to cling and grasp, control and manipulate, fix and fill in order to numb the pain of that separateness. Such moments are tastes of eternity that make me long for more of eternity; oftentimes the longing is so painful that tears come.

But in solitude there is rest from all of that, and for a time it is as if I come in touch with a deep current of truth that runs underneath everything else: All things have already been reconciled in Christ—even those people and things that seem broken beyond repair. In solitude I know that even those things that seem irreconcilable are somehow reconciled in Christ. Everything is already one through the person and work of Christ in the timelessness that is God. When I am in solitude, the presence of God is so real and so full that there is nothing else I want. The people I love are with me in God's presence, beyond the surface choppiness of all the stresses that separate us as finite beings on this earth, and I am able to experience our ultimate togetherness in God. This experience is absolutely the only thing that fills the longing of my heart.

When I reengage my life in community with others and live *from that place of union with God,* there is indeed a peace that passes understanding and transcends the longing. The longing is still there, but the longing is not ultimate. It is God who is ultimate, and all of us are in God. Maybe nothing in my external world has changed, but I have changed, and that is what the people around me need more than anything.

I wish I could explain it better, but this is what I know.

✺ PRACTICE

Choose a place that feels comfortable and safe to you, a place that allows you to be open and available to God—a favorite chair at home, your own backyard if it is quiet, or even a nearby chapel if you have access to one.

Settle into a comfortable position in your body and sit quietly for a few moments, breathing deeply, becoming aware of God's presence with you and your desire to be present with God.

Sit quietly at the base of the tree that is your life and begin to notice what is true about you these days. Don't rush or try to make anything happen. Let your soul venture out and say something to you that perhaps you have had a hard time acknowledging: Is there a particular joy you are celebrating? A loss you are grieving? Are there tears that have been waiting to be shed? A question that is stirring? An emotion that needs expression?

Sit with what comes into your awareness, becoming conscious of

"The fact is there is nothing that we are doing that God could not raise up a stone in the field to do for him. The realization of this puts us in our true place. Though, lest we get too knocked down by such a realization of our insignificance, let me hasten to add that there is one thing that we alone can give God . . . and that is our personal love. No one else can give God our personal love. This is our great significance."

M. BASIL PENNINGTON,
FINDING GRACE AT THE CENTER

God's presence with you in that awareness. Don't try to do anything with what you are knowing except be with it. (In other words, don't scare it away.) Feel the difference between trying to fix it and just being with it. Feel the difference between doing something with it and resting with it. Feel the difference between trying to fight it and letting God fight for you. What does it mean for you to *be still and let God fight (or work) for you* in this particular area?

Practice this way of entering into solitude regularly until it becomes routine for you to begin your times in solitude by being quiet and letting your soul come out and then rest in God's presence. You will likely be surprised at what your soul wants to say to God.

There are many other ways of being with God in solitude which we will explore later, but for now take time to allow this ability to rest in God become the foundation of your times in solitude.

3

SCRIPTURE

Encountering God Through *Lectio Divina*

The Word of Scripture should never stop sounding in your ears and
working in you all day long, just like the words of someone you love.
And just as you do not analyze the words of someone you love, but
accept them as they are said to you, accept the Word of Scripture and
ponder it in your heart, as Mary did. That is all. . . . Do not ask
"How shall I pass this on?" but "What does it say to me?" Then ponder
this word long in your heart until it has gone right into you and taken
possession of you.

DIETRICH BONHOEFFER, *LIFE TOGETHER*

I must confess that at times I have real feelings of ambivalence about
the Scriptures. From my earliest days in church and in Sunday school, I
learned that the Scriptures are God breathed and that they are alive, active and sharper than any two-edged sword. They are God's words to us,
intended to bring us life. And at times all of these things have been true
for me.

I will never forget the excitement I felt after giving my life to Christ at
a summer youth camp just before entering ninth grade. Although I had
"asked Jesus to come into my heart" during family devotions when I was
just four years old, that summer's encounter was my first real conversion
experience. For the first time I acknowledged my sinfulness and rebel-

lion against God (and my parents!) and "turned around," leaving one way of life for another. This was my first experience of the kind of self-awareness that leads to godly grief and then repentance. The Scriptures were alive to me, and I craved them because they led to tangible changes in my attitudes and behaviors. (Just ask my parents!)

I had quiet times before I even knew they were a requirement for Christian living. I would take my Bible and a journal, sometimes a Bible study guide or a book of poetry, find a private corner and lose myself in it all. The Psalms in particular were amazing to me. They were full of the same rampage of emotions that I was experiencing as an adolescent— anger and sadness, loneliness and questions, yearning and passion, worship and awe. When I was immersed in the Psalms I felt understood and comforted—as if Someone really *got* me. And when I read David's confessions of his sin with Bathsheba or his seething hatred of his enemies, I knew there was nothing I couldn't name in God's presence. Nothing was out of bounds.

For a passionate, melancholy young girl who was being raised in a very conservative religious environment, this was no small thing. The Scriptures gave me a place to be and to breathe. I loved God because of what I learned about God from the Scriptures.

When I graduated from high school and went to Bible college at (barely) seventeen years of age, a whole new world opened up: the world of serious Bible study. And I do mean *serious* Bible study, beyond devotional approaches to Scripture and application-oriented youth messages. I discovered that you could study Scripture like a textbook and it would hold up under scrutiny. You could study it from different angles: as a history book, as a compilation of great literature, as a tool for developing systematic theologies, as a sociology text that illustrates various facets of the human condition. It was even a place to encounter a couple of different and very intriguing languages, if you were into that sort of thing. And I was!

I was introduced to the most amazing words for categorizing biblical themes—words like *theology, pneumatology, soteriology, christology, eschatology, hermeneutics.* It made me feel important just to be able to use such words and know what they meant. This was pretty heady stuff for a teenager!

I also discovered the joy of using Scripture to help others. There was a whole new kind of exhilaration that came from working hard to grasp biblical truth, finding a way to frame it logically and creatively, and then sharing it with others in a way that actually helped them. This was the beginning of my life in Christian ministry, a life of studying, teaching and applying Scripture, and it was deeply satisfying.

To a point.

You see, something else was happening that was very subtle. Somewhere along the way I figured out that you could get really good at studying and memorizing verses, filling in the blanks of Bible study guides, checking chapters off a reading list, coming up with creative approaches for Bible study and message preparation. In my circles, you could get major brownie points for such things. Although I wouldn't have known how to talk about it then, slowly but surely the Scriptures were becoming a place of human striving and intellectual hard work. Somehow, I had fallen into a pattern of using the Scriptures as a tool to accomplish utilitarian purposes rather experiencing them primarily as a place of intimacy with God for my own soul's sake.

And somewhere along the way I got tired. Very tired. When I was alone with the Scriptures, they began to feel lifeless and boring, irrelevant and obligatory. When I was with the Scriptures with others—in Bible studies, listening to sermons, reading books and commentaries—the Scriptures felt ponderous, like a tool people were using to rein me in, or tell me what to do, or coerce me into their way of thinking.

This kind of admission doesn't go over very well in your average church setting or small group Bible study, but it was true nonetheless.

The real surprise was not that this happened but the fact that the shift was so subtle. After all, the purposes for which I was using the Scriptures were not bad in and of themselves. It's just that over time, without my awareness, those purposes had trumped the greater purpose for which the Scriptures have been given: to allow my own heart and soul to be penetrated by an intimate word from God. My mind remained engaged, but my heart and soul had drifted far away.

✺ READING FOR INFORMATION OR TRANSFORMATION?

One way to reflect on our varied experiences with Scripture is to think about the difference between reading a newspaper or textbook and reading a love letter. Think about how you read the newspaper this morning. You probably read it hurriedly to get the highlights of what is going on in our world ("just the facts, ma'am"). You might have taken it with a grain of salt, not convinced that everything you read was totally factual and unbiased. You probably did some picking and choosing of what was interesting or pertinent to you and didn't even finish most of the articles. My guess is that you probably did not feel a whole lot of anticipation as you picked up the paper this morning, because much of the news is bad news and it is not intended to produce a deep emotional experience anyway. Chances are you didn't notice who wrote the articles, nor did you even care.

It is the same with a textbook. If you think back to your high school or college days, you probably remember at times employing techniques that enabled you to read as little as possible to get the best grade possible—particularly when it was a subject that didn't interest you. In such cases, most of us got pretty good at cramming information into our head and keeping it there just long enough to be able to regurgitate it on a test. There was no emotional connection with the author or the content. While there were (thankfully) courses that we loved, there were also those times when we had specific and very utilitarian purposes in mind as we read—getting a good grade, being able to check a reading assignment off a list, solving a problem or proving a point, writing a book report—and when that purpose was accomplished, we didn't think of it again.

Now, perhaps you can remember a time when you were exchanging love letters with someone. Do you remember the sense of anticipation you had when you opened a letter? Can you recall how wonderful it was to have this special person express their feelings for you? Do you remember where you would go to read the letter—perhaps a quiet, private place—and how you savored each and every word and pondered what these things might mean? What emotions did you feel? Do you still have those letters tucked away in some special place to remind you of that special person and that special time?

The sad truth is that many of us approach the Scriptures more like a textbook than like a love letter. In Western culture in particular, we are predisposed to a certain kind of reading. We have been schooled in an informational reading process that establishes the reader as the master of the text. As the reader, I employ key techniques that allow me to use the text to advance my own purposes. With this kind of reading, the intent is to cover as much ground as possible as quickly as possible. Our emphasis is primarily on mastery, that is, controlling the text for our own ends—gathering information, interpreting or applying the information, proving our point about something, gaining a ministry tool or solving a problem.

When we are in an information-gathering mindset, we are analytical in our approach and at times even critical and judgmental. We are reading through cognitive filters, made up of our preconceived thoughts, feelings, biases, doctrinal systems, teachings and life experiences that have shaped us. When we are in this mode, it is exceedingly difficult for us to hear anything new because we have so many unconscious defenses in place.

The information-gathering mindset is very appropriate and helpful for a student in an academic or a learning environment. But when applied to Scripture, this approach does not serve the deeper longing of our heart— the longing to hear a word from God that is personal and intimate and takes us deeper into the love that our soul craves. The study of Scripture is important, but if we stop there, we will eventually hit a wall spiritually. Information gathering may be exhilarating and even useful at times, but in the end our soul knows that there must be something more.

READING FOR RELATIONSHIP

When we engage the Scriptures for spiritual transformation, on the other hand, we engage not only our mind but also our heart, our emotions, our body, our curiosity, our imagination and our will. We open ourselves to a deeper level of understanding and insight that grows out of and leads us deeper into our personal relationship with the One behind the text. And it is in the context of relational intimacy that real life change takes place.

This is a fundamentally different kind of engagement than what we are normally accustomed to with the things we read. When we engage the Scriptures for spiritual transformation, we make it our top priority to listen to God relationally rather than seeking only to learn more about God cognitively. Our approach is driven by the longing of a lover. We read slowly so that we can savor each word and let its meaning sink in. Rather than rushing on to the next chapter so that we can complete a reading or study assignment, we stay in the place where God is speaking to us, contemplating its meaning for our life and for our relationship. We receive it as it is given without judgment, wanting only to hear the heart of this One we love. Like the little boy Samuel, we approach the Scripture with utter openness and availability to God: "Speak, LORD, for your servant is listening" (1 Samuel 3:9).

In this listening stance, Scripture becomes an instrument of God's control rather than a tool that we control to our own ends. Then, as God speaks to us through Scripture, we respond to what we read with our heart and soul rather that just our intellect. When we are falling in love with someone, we want to know everything about them. We are fascinated by every detail, every relationship and every event that shaped them. But the desire for intimacy moves us beyond fact finding to seeking understanding, connecting with that person emotionally and sensing our own response. Thus when we read Scripture for relationship we pay attention to our own inner dynamics and allow our response to take place in the deeper levels of our beings. We are open to a whole different set of questions—questions that help us to risk greater levels of truth telling with ourselves and with God. In addition to asking, *What does it say? What does it mean? How do I apply it to my life?*—all questions that promote primarily cognitive activity and allow us to remain firmly in control of the whole experience—we might ask:

- How do I feel about what is being said? Where do I find myself resonating deeply? Where do I find myself resisting, pulling back, wrestling with what Scripture might be saying? (Note: It is important to notice these inner dynamics *without judging them,* because they have much to tell us. You may even notice that you feel resonance and resistance at the same time. For instance, you may have a deep sense of the rightness of what the text is saying but on another level have the feeling *There is no way I can do that!* This is a particularly important dynamic to notice, because it indicates a place where God is at work beyond your own cognition.)

- Why do I feel this way? What aspect of my life or my inner being is being touched or spoken to through this Scripture?

- What do my reactions tell me about myself—my attitudes, my relating patterns, my perspectives, my behaviors? Am I willing to look at that in God's presence?

✒ MOVING FROM HEAD TO HEART

Allowing ourselves to pay attention at this level may feel a bit threatening at first, depending on how suspicious or out of touch we are with our feelings and other internal dynamics. Robert Mulholland points out that in our culture there is generally little danger of neglecting the cognitive, rational, analytical dynamics of our being, for these

> are so hyper-developed in our culture and in our normal modes of learning that we are not going to have to worry about getting them out of balance. . . . Yes, we must love God with all of our mind . . . however, we must remember that the injunction to love God with all of our mind comes a little further down the road in Jesus' list; loving God with all of our heart and all of our soul precedes loving God with all of our mind.

Something powerfully different happens when we are willing to pay attention to our internal dynamics rather than just reading for information or reading to complete the assigned reading for the day. Say I have chosen a reading program that requires me to read three to five chapters a day in order to read through the Bible in a year. As I follow the program, I come across the passage in Luke 6 where Jesus talks about loving our enemies as a mark of true Christianity. This is a pretty basic concept that most of us learned in our earliest days in Sunday school, and so it feels fairly routine. If I am trying to get through the allotted number of chapters for the day, chances are I will keep charging through the passage so I can check it off the list.

If, on the other hand, I am seeking to engage the Scriptures for spiritual transformation, I may also set aside some time to read a shorter passage (six to eight verses perhaps) that I feel drawn to. I savor the words and wonder what is on God's heart for me today. I have no other agenda except listening and deepening my intimacy with God, so I can take time to notice that when I read Luke 6:27 and the following verses I feel a bit resistant. It's pretty subtle at first, but I stop and give myself a little space to notice that feeling and wonder about it. Lo and behold, it proves to be more than a vague feeling of discomfort. There is a fist rising up from my gut that says, *I don't think so!* And I am caught completely off guard, because I had been feeling pretty spiritual when I began my Bible reading for the day.

But rather than judging myself (which I am prone to do), I wonder what aspect of myself or my life is being touched by this verse. As I sit with my resistance, I realize that underneath all my piety, there is a part of me that is not feeling very loving at all today. In fact, I am harboring real anger toward someone who has hurt me. I thought I had put it to rest, but on this day, in response to this verse, I realize that the anger is still alive and well. I can see the perpetrator in my mind's eye, the details are crystal clear along with the injustice of it all, and I feel the anger all over again. No wonder there is something in me that rises up and fights or resists. If *that* is the person I am supposed to love, then *I don't think so!*

Now if I choose to, I can reflect more deeply on what my reactions tell me about myself. How am I doing with the issue of love in my life— really? What does this particular awareness on this day tell me about where I am not like Christ? Am I being transformed into a more loving person—even in the most challenging of situations—or am I harboring places of bitterness where my spirit is closed? What does this tell me about my spiritual condition? Am I willing to look at that in God's presence?

Now we're talkin'! Now God and I are having a conversation that has some substance to it! This is the level at which intimacy unfolds in a way that has the potential to change me in the deepest places of my being.

It reminds me of how the desert fathers read Scriptures. For them, contact with Scripture was "contact with fire that burns, disturbs, calls violently to conversion." The story is told of someone coming to Abba Pambo, asking him to teach him a psalm. Pambo begins to teach him Psalm 39, but hardly has he pronounced the first verse, "I will be watchful of my ways, for fear I should sin with my tongue," when the brother said he does not wish to hear anymore. He tells Pambo, "This verse is enough for me; please God may I have the strength to learn it and put it into practice." Nineteen years later he was still trying.

ENCOUNTERING GOD IN SCRIPTURE

Right about now you may be feeling one of several different emotions. You may be aware of a longing to experience the Scripture in the way that was just described. And while your heart beats fast to think that you may be able to encounter God in Scripture, you know that it's going to take a lot more than a few new questions to satisfy your longing. Perhaps you are cautiously optimistic about finding a more life-giving way of approaching Scripture; however, you also have a dawning awareness of how deeply ingrained your information-grasping patterns are, and you wonder how in the world you can shift them. You don't know whether to be hopeful or to give in to despair.

All of this is true. We need a way of approaching Scripture that will move us *very* concretely from our overreliance on information gathering to an experience of Scripture as a place of intimate encounter. We need more than a method or a technique that involves asking a different set of questions. We need a different way of being with Scripture that allows God to initiate with us (beyond all the ways we seek to control such things) and also creates space for us to respond fully (beyond all the ways we hold ourselves so tight). *Lectio divina* provides us with just such a way.

Lectio divina (translated "divine [or sacred] reading") is an approach to the Scriptures that sets us up to listen for the word of God spoken to us in the present moment. *Lectio divina* is a practice of divine reading that dates back to the early mothers and fathers of the Christian faith. Referring to the material being read and the method itself, the practice of *lectio divina* is rooted in the belief that through the presence of the Holy Spirit, the Scriptures are indeed alive and active as we engage them for spiritual transformation (Hebrews 4:12).

As we make ourselves open and available to God through this practice, the Scriptures will penetrate to our very depths, showing us those things about ourselves that we are incapable of knowing on our own due to our well-developed defense structures. In the context of such radical self-knowledge, God will invite us into our next steps with him or touch us with his healing grace. Invariably he communicates his love for us in ways that we can hear and experience beyond cognitive knowing.

One of the reasons this approach is so powerful is that *lectio divina* involves a delicate balance of silence and word. It is a very concrete way of entering into the rhythm of speaking and listening involved in intimate communication. It incorporates several spiritual practices that support and catalyze life-transforming relationship with God. A period of silence before the reading of Scripture helps us to quiet our inner chaos so that we are prepared to listen. After we read Scripture, silence helps us be attentive to God when he does speak and creates space for noticing our inner dynamics and exploring them in God's presence.

Lectio involves a slower, more reflective reading of Scripture that helps us to be open to God's initiative rather than being subject to human agendas—our own or someone else's. It also allows for at least two different kinds of prayer that are not heavy-laden with human effort. One is a prayer of response. This is prayer that most naturally flows out of what we've heard or sensed is God's invitation to us. *Lectio divina* offers the space for this kind of response to flow, which is a very intimate thing. It also incorporates the prayer of rest—prayer beyond words in which we rest in God's love and sovereignty in our life. This is a great way to conclude any experience with Scripture, and again, it is built right into the process.

Although Bible study is not a part of the *lectio* process itself, Bible study is an essential supplement to it. *Lectio* can actually be used as a powerful follow-up to more traditional Bible study methods, moving people very naturally into the process of application. (An excellent source for helping us experience the interplay between Bible study and *lectio divina* is *Contemplative Bible Reading* by Richard Peace.)

✷ EXPLORING THE PROCESS OF *LECTIO DIVINA*

Lectio divina is experienced in four movements. We might think of them as moves rather than steps because it reminds us of dancing. When we are first learning a new dance, we are very awkward and very concerned about getting it right. We watch our feet, trying to get them to do what they are supposed to do. We wonder what to do with our hands. If we are dancing with a partner, we may be clumsy at first as we try to figure out how to move together gracefully. But in the end, the point is to be able to enter into the dance, flow with it, improvise and enjoy the person we are dancing with.

It is the same with *lectio divina*. When we are just starting out, we concentrate on following the steps and getting everything in the right order. But eventually as we become more comfortable, they become moves in a dance that flows with beauty and pleasure, heart and soul. The moves become very fluid and flow into one another quite naturally. But first we do have to familiarize ourselves with the basic moves.

To prepare for the *lectio* process, we first choose a passage of Scripture no more than six to eight verses in length. We begin with a time of silent preparation (*silencio*) in which we become quiet in God's presence and touch our desire to hear from God. This gives us the opportunity to allow the busyness and chaos of our life to settle down until there is a quiet inner space in which we can hear from God.

Then we read the chosen passage four consecutive times, each time asking a different question that invites us into the dynamic of that move. Each reading is followed by a brief period of silence.

The first move is *to read* (*lectio*). In this move, we read the passage once or even twice, listening for the word or the phrase that strikes us. This word somehow stands out from all the rest, causes a visceral reaction or brings about a deep sense of resonance or resistance, The mood is gentle, reflective, and we have a sense of expectancy that God will speak to us. After the reading there is a brief period of silence in which we remain with the word, savoring it and repeating it without trying to figure out what it means or why it was given.

The second move is *to reflect (meditatio)*. We read the passage a second time, and this time we reflect on the way our life is touched by this word. We might ask, *What is it in my life that needed to hear this word today?* Or, if the passage is a story: *Where am I in this text, and what do I experience as I allow myself to be in this story?* Again, there is a brief period of silence in which we stay present with God with whatever comes. Rather than thinking too much about the passage (and we have to be very careful here), we keep coming back to the word that we have been given.

The third move is *to respond (oratio)*. Is there an invitation or a challenge for us to respond to? What is our response to God's invitation? This is the first and unedited response to what we have heard. It is the prayer that comes most naturally in response to what we have heard God say to us, and we allow it to flow freely in the moments of silence that follow. Perhaps Scripture has touched a place of pain, frustration or anger, and we pour out these feelings in the safety of this moment. Perhaps there is a flash of self-knowledge, and we are convicted of some sin. In the silence we feel our remorse and make our confession. Perhaps we are overwhelmed by some way in which God tells us that he

> *When our response has been played out in all of its fury, angst, or exuberance, we come to a place of rest in God. Here there are no expectations, demands, no need to know, no desire but to be in the Divine Presence, receptive to what God desires to do with us.*
>
> MARJORIE THOMPSON,
> *SOULFEAST*

loves us, and in the silence we let tears of love and gratitude flow and just soak in God's love. Or perhaps we hear God calling us to something new, and our heart exclaims, "You've got to be kidding!" Whatever our response, we let it find full expression in the silence.

When our response has subsided, we read the passage one last time, and this time the invitation is *contemplatio*—to rest in God. We are like the weaned child in Psalm 131 who has received what it needs from its mother and can now rest with her in peace and quiet. Here we rest with God and enjoy his presence, realizing that God is the One who will enable us to respond faithfully to whatever invitation we have heard from him. We resolve to carry this word with us and live it out *(incarnatio)* in our daily life. We continue to listen to it throughout the day as we are led deeper and deeper into its meaning and it begins to live in us.

✎ THE POWER OF *LECTIO DIVINA*

Lectio is a delightful discipline and one on which so many books have been written that I pray I have not misrepresented its depth by presenting it so simply. The power, of course, is in the doing.

Though *lectio* was originally developed as a private discipline, my first experience with *lectio divina* was in a small group setting at a conference, with teaching and facilitation by Richard Peace. Richard was to read a chosen passage from the front of the room. After every move—the reading and then the silence—we were to go around the circle in our small groups and share very briefly what we had just experienced. Most of us didn't know each other, and that didn't matter at all: the purpose of the group was to support each one of us as we listened to God in Scripture in a very personal way within this small community.

The passage Richard chose was Matthew 14:22-32, the story of Peter walking to Jesus on the water. A very familiar story. There would have been little a speaker could have said on that passage that would have been new to me. But as Richard read the passage aloud for the first time,

I was pierced. One word was much louder and clearer than all the rest: *Come.* I knew this was the word, because as I heard it I felt both resistance in my gut and resonance in my heart. It was the strangest and most compelling experience with Scripture I had ever had.

In the first move, I heard the word clearly and couldn't make any sense of it, so I sat with it. In the second move, I started to get an inkling of the place in my life where God was asking me to risk more to be faithful to his call. And in the third move, I could hear myself saying to God, "But I have come as far as I can! I can't come any further!" Yet even as I was protesting, I could feel great warmth and desire—the same desire that must have led Peter to jump out of the boat. I wanted so much to go to Jesus on the water! As frightened as I felt, I was thrilled at the idea that maybe there was more ahead for me. I was so glad that Jesus wanted me to come to him and that he was inviting me.

This was an extremely intimate moment with God, a time of wrestling but also of longing and joy and giving myself over to him in a new way. And sure enough, shortly thereafter I faced a new challenge that required courage, and Jesus' word *Come* was exactly the word I needed. In this moment I understood afresh that the Scripture is truly unlike any other book on the planet. It is alive and it is God breathed, not just way back when it was written but now, each and every time I find ways to open myself to its power.

✥ PRACTICE

Choose a passage (six to eight verses); it can be part of your normal reading plan, a passage you select for today or a passage from the lectionary reading for this week. Use it to enter prayerfully into the *lectio* process. Following are very detailed instructions to help you learn the moves.

Preparation (*Silencio*). Take a moment to come fully into the present. With your eyes closed, let your body relax, and allow yourself to become consciously aware of God's presence with you. Express your willingness (or your willingness to be made willing) to hear from God in these moments by using a brief prayer such as "Come Lord Jesus," or "Here I am," or "Speak, Lord, for your servant is listening."

Read (Lectio): Listen for the word or the phrase that is addressed to you. Turn to the passage and begin to read slowly, pausing between phrases and sentences. You may read silently, or you may find it helpful to read the passage aloud, allowing the words to echo and resonate, sink in and settle into your heart. As you read, listen for a word or phrase that strikes you or catches your attention. Allow a moment of silence, repeating that word or phrase softly to yourself, pondering it and savoring it as though pondering the words of a loved one. This is the word that is meant for you. Be content to listen simply and openly, without judging or analyzing.

Reflect (Meditatio): How is my life touched by this word? Once you have heard the word that is meant for you, read the passage again, and listen for the way this passage connects with your life. Ask, *What is it in my life right now that needs to hear this word?* Allow several moments of silence following this reading, and explore thoughts, perceptions and sensory impressions. If the passage is a story, perhaps ask yourself, *Where am I in this scene? What do I hear as I imagine myself in the story or hear these words addressed specifically to me? How do the dynamics of this story connect with my own life experience?*

Respond (Oratio): What is my response to God based on what I have read and encountered? Read the passage one more time, listening for your own deepest and truest response. In silence after the reading, allow your prayer to flow spontaneously from your heart as fully and as truly as you can. At this point you are entering into a personal dialogue with God, "sharing with God the feelings the text has aroused, . . . feelings such as love, joy, sorrow, anger, repentance, desire, need, conviction, consecration. We pour out our hearts in complete honesty, especially as the text has probed aspects of our being and doing in the midst of various issues and relationships." Pay attention to any sense that God is inviting you to act or to respond in some way to the word you have heard. You may find it helpful to write your prayers or to journal at this point.

Rest *(Contemplatio): Rest in the Word of God.* In this final reading you are invited to release and return to a place of rest in God. You have given your response its full expression, so now you can move into a time of waiting and resting in God's presence, like the weaned child who leans against its mother (Psalm 131:2). This is a posture of total yieldedness and abandon to the great Lover of your soul.

Resolve *(Incarnatio): Incarnate (live out) the Word of God.* As you emerge from this place of personal encounter with God to life in the company of others, resolve to carry this word with you and to live it out in the context of daily life and activity. As you continue to listen to the word throughout the day, you will be led deeper and deeper into its meaning, until it begins to live in you and you *enflesh* this word to the world in which you live. As a way of supporting your intent to live out the word you have been given, you may want to choose an image, a picture or a symbol that you can carry to remind you of it.

4

PRAYER

Deepening Our Intimacy with God

*Prayer is like love. Words pour at first. Then we are more silent
and can communicate in monosyllables. In difficulties a gesture is
enough, a word, or nothing at all—love is enough. Thus the time
comes when words are superfluous. . . . The soul converses with God
with a single loving glance, although this may often be accompanied
by dryness and suffering.*

CARLO CARRETTO

Spring has finally come to Chicago, and today, in the midst of writing,
I have been pining for beauty and color. And so, even though it is a bit
early in the season, I have planted flowers. Pansies to be exact. Deep pur-
ple. Bright yellow. The colors of Easter, a friend reminds me. Thanks be
to God.

As I pull the vibrant clumps of color out of the plastic cells where they
have been cultivated for selling, I notice a familiar phenomenon: the
plastic containers are packed with roots. There is little to no dirt left in
the containers, and some of the roots are even dangling through the water holes, desperately searching for water and nutrients. I wrestle the
flowers carefully from their tight, overcrowded holders, careful to do it
gently enough that I don't mangle them or rip them from their roots. Part
of the pleasure of it all is setting them in a larger space where there is

fresh dirt and room for the root system to spread out, and knowing that this spaciousness will produce mounds of flowers throughout the season. I imagine that the pansies are relieved to be released from such cramped quarters, and I am pleased.

It is the same with the human soul. Like a plant that has become pot-bound, its roots searching for nutrients that have long since been used up, the human soul gets to the point when it is ready for a more spacious way to pray, one that provides more room for the mystery of growth in intimacy with God and more depth for the roots to sink into. The forms of prayer that were preferred and taught in the context of our religious upbringing or in the early days of our Christian experience no longer contain our experience of God or take us any further in our quest for intimacy with God. We long for something more.

✎ BEGINNING AGAIN

One thing I know for sure about prayer these days is that we do not know how to pray. It is only the young in Christ who think they know how to pray; the rest of us know we are just beginners.So let's try to begin together, which is really all we can do.

Simply put, prayer is *all the ways in which we communicate and commune with God.* The fundamental purpose of prayer is to deepen our intimacy with God. Early in the spiritual life we experience this intimacy primarily through the words we say *to* God, and there is deep satisfaction in it.

> Words pour out to begin with. . . . Mostly a soul speaks a great deal at the time of its conversion, during the period of its novitiate, that is, the first years of its discovery of God. It is the easiest time for the soul. Prayer has a certain novelty; it seizes the imagination. And God, for his part, encourages the soul; everything pours out as in the beginning of a happy marriage.
>
> In the next stage, we need to know what others have said about God,

so we study a lot and reflect deeply on theological truth. This is a time of great joy and great reward, when many things about God seem clear and our response is glad service. It is good to receive and enjoy these gifts for as long as they are available to us.

But eventually there comes a time when prayer just doesn't work as it used to. Our intellectual considerations of the mystery of God and our wordy responses no longer feel very satisfying. For a while we may try to work harder at prayer the way we have always known it, or we may try to find a better method, but no matter how much effort we put into it or how faithful we are, nothing happens. While we have surely experienced times of dryness before, they always seemed to pass, and experiences of intimacy with God would return. But this time is different. This time we seem to have no control over what does or does not happen in our life with God.

This is very traumatic for the tender soul and may send us spiraling into doubt about our spirituality, wondering if we have completely lost our way. As time goes by, we may even become angry at God for not making himself known to us in ways that are as "knowable" as they were before—especially since we are trying so hard to be faithful. Confusion and questions about how to connect with God set in, and the emptiness seems too much to bear. We wonder if we have somehow fallen off the spiritual path. *There has to be more to the spiritual life than this!* the soul cries out in deep disillusionment. The ability to pray eludes us, and for the first time we know—really *know*—that we do not know how to pray as we ought.

A Deeper Invitation

The experience of having our prayers go cold, as distressing as it is, signals a major transition in the life of prayer and thus in our relationship with God. It signals an invitation to deeper levels of intimacy that will move us beyond *communication*, which primarily involves words and concepts, into *communion,* which is primarily beyond words. If there are any words at all, they are reduced to the simplest and most visceral expressions.

In Christian tradition, there are several signs that indicate we are transitioning into a new phase in the life of prayer:

1. What you are doing isn't working, no matter how much effort you put into it. You find yourself asking, *Is this all there is?*

2. Your desire for God continues to be strong even though you have no desire for anything external—words, images, previous structures for prayer, including the Scriptures. While these things may still be present to some extent, you are not attracted to them anymore. Words fail. The hunger for intimacy—to just hang out with God—is all there is.

3. You find yourself enjoying being alone, aware of God's presence without structured activity. In the deepest part of your being, you know that God alone can satisfy the longings of the human heart, and other things fade in importance. There is no attraction to thought, meditation, or any other human activity or achievement. This last condition is most important, for it justifies the other two and indicates a readiness to leave words behind and remain with God alone in an act of love.

This transitional place in the life of prayer can be frightening, because it requires us to let go of what we have known in order to open ourselves to something new. It can feel as if we are being ripped from the safety and familiarity of a known space and our roots are dangling in midair. Whereas the old space held us snugly and we felt secure there, now we are being transplanted to a space that is less protected and less structured. We are left feeling vulnerable and unsure, like a tender sapling exposed to the wind and the elements.

✺ PRAYER AS INTIMACY

This deeper invitation is unsettling for another reason as well. It requires letting go *into* that relational free-fall that we call intimacy, giving ourselves fully and openly and vulnerably to another. And the truth is, most of us have at least some ambivalence about intimacy; we cry out for intimacy with God, but we resist it at the very same time. In most cases, the reason we prefer to talk *about* prayer and read *about* prayer but don't actually pray has more to do with our ambivalence about intimacy than with anything else. Why does this ambivalence arise?

Instinctively we know that intimacy requires something of us. One of the most consistent metaphors in Scripture for God's relationship with us is God as an intimate lover—a jealous lover, even. Sometimes Scripture's language describing God's love for us and pursuit of us is erotic and passionate. Sometimes it is emotional and gut wrenching. Other times it is quiet and tender or plaintive and haunting. Always it engages all of who we are.

> When we read God's story in the Old and New Testaments we are confronted with a God who is always after us, looking for us, and who cries out each time he finds us with a divine despair. . . . He wants us here, now, totally, unconditionally. As long as we continue to reduce prayer to occasional piety we keep running away from the mystery of God's jealous love. . . . Looking at prayer as a generous response to a jealous God helps explain why we may have serious reservations about prayer. . . . Prayer means letting God's creative love touch the most hidden places of our being and prayer means listening with attentive, undivided hearts to the inner movement of the Spirit of Jesus, even when that Spirit leads us to places we would rather not go.

Intimacy also requires risk—the risk of allowing someone to see me in my nakedness and vulnerability as well as in my strength and beauty. The dynamics that accompany the nakedness and vulnerability required for sexual intimacy are the very dynamics the soul experiences as it moves deeper into spiritual intimacy with God. It involves bringing more and more of myself into God's presence and receiving more and more of God's being into myself.

Perhaps the deepest reason we are ambivalent about the intimacy of true prayer is that intimacy always leads us to a place where we are not in control. When we give ourselves over to another person in the act of love, we are not in control. When we give our heart and our life to another in committed friendship or marriage, we know that we give them the ability to do us great good or great harm. While we choose our intimate ones as wisely as we can, there are no guarantees. We can never fully control another human being.

Our patterns of intimacy or nonintimacy with other human beings are the very same patterns we bring to our relationship with God, whether we are conscious of it or not. Depending on what our previous experiences with intimacy have been, relinquishing control can be difficult or even impossible. If we have a high need to be in control in our human relationships (and most of us do), intimacy with God will be very challenging for us. If we are afraid of intimacy or hold ourselves back in human relationships, that will be our pattern with God as well.

Prayer gives form to our quest for deeper levels of intimacy with God, providing us with a path for moving beyond our ambivalence.

PRAYER BEYOND WORDS

If we let go of what's not working, we can begin to acknowledge that wordy prayers fail to capture the depths of our longing for God, the emptiness we feel in the absence of the soul's normal consolations, the darkness of not knowing. The effort to capture these depths in words feels difficult, if not impossible, like a violation of something that is deeply intimate. We are almost afraid that the experience will dissipate if we try to impose words on it. At this point prayer is much less about technique and much more about the beyond-words intimacy that is developing in our relationship with God.

There are many terms that seek to capture this dynamic—*silent prayer, centering prayer, contemplative prayer, interior prayer, prayer of the heart.* Each one carries a slightly different nuance, but they all are attempts to capture the same thing: the movement beyond words to an intimacy that requires no words. This intimacy is the kind that lovers know when they give themselves over to the act of lovemaking, the kind a mother experiences with a nursing baby, the kind that intimate friends know when they have said all there is to say and settle into a comfortable silence, content to just be in each other's presence. If you have had the joy of any of these experiences, you know that this is much more intimate than the noisy chatter that usually fills our social interactions. This silent "being with" is full and satisfying.

The reason this kind of prayer is so satisfying is that it is about knowing God experientially rather than just knowing a lot *about* God. The Greek word *epiginōskō* implies an intimate knowledge involving the whole person, not just the mind. This kind of knowledge perfectly unites the subject with the object, and it can be attained only by entering into a love relationship. The apostle John's leaning against Jesus' chest at the Last Supper is a poignant picture of this kind of love and intimacy. Even by today's standard, the intimacy pictured here between John and Jesus is striking and compelling: two people who are comfortable enough with each other to commune beyond words. One gets the impression that this intimacy was so satisfying for John that he was almost disinterested in the wordy conversation that was going on around him.

The Old Testament also refers repeatedly to a kind of knowing that comes in the absence of words or in the stillness of waiting. *Be still before the Lord and wait. Be still and know that I am God. In silence my soul waits for you and you alone, oh God.*

This is a prayer of self-emptying that enables us to receive whatever it is that God wants to give. We come to him with empty hands and empty heart, having no agenda. Half the time we don't even know what we need; we just come with a sense of our own spiritual poverty. "Blessed are the poor in spirit, for theirs is the kingdom of heaven" (Matthew 5:3). Emptiness is the prerequisite for receiving.

The story is told of a learned professor who went to visit an old monk who was famous for his wisdom. The monk graciously welcomed him into his temple and offered him a seat on a cushion. No sooner had the professor sat down than he launched into a long, wordy account of his own accomplishments, his own knowledge, his own theories and opinions. The monk listened quietly for awhile and then asked politely, "Would you like some tea?"

The professor nodded, smiled and kept right on talking. The monk handed him a teacup and began pouring tea from a large pot. The tea rose to the brim of the cup, but the monk kept right on pouring while the professor kept right on talking. Finally the professor noticed what was going on, leaped to his feet and demanded, "What are you doing? Can't you see that the cup is overflowing?"

To which the monk replied, "This cup is like your mind. It can't take in anything new because it's already full."

How can we possibly expect anyone to find real nurture, comfort and consolation from a prayer life that taxes the mind beyond its limits and adds one more exhausting activity to the many already scheduled ones?

HENRI J. M. NOUWEN,
THE WAY OF THE HEART

Eventually, when we stop the flow of our own words, another gift comes to us, quietly and imperceptibly at first: we find ourselves resting in prayer. Rather than working so hard to put everything into words, we rest from the noise and stimulation that are so characteristic of life in our culture. We rest our overactive, hardworking mind from the need to put everything into words. We rest from clinging, grasping and trying to figure everything out. The soul returns to its most natural state in God. *In returning and rest you will be saved.*

✎ THE INTIMACY OF BREATHING

In the stillness we make yet another discovery: the Holy Spirit is the One who really knows how to pray. We discover that prayer is truest when it has passed beyond words into the realm where the Holy Spirit groans for us with utterances that are too deep for words (see Romans 8:26-27). The silence becomes a time when we listen for the prayer that the Holy Spirit is praying deep within us as he moves between the depths of our human experience and the divine will, interceding for us beyond words.

Words, when they do find their way to the surface from these depths, carry with them a whole new power and meaning because they are forged in the caldron of our deepest longings for God.

> In this period, the so-called litanical prayer thrives: that is, repetition of identical expressions, poor words but very rich in content . . . Jesus I love you . . . Lord have mercy on me . . . my God and my all. And it is strange how in these ejaculations, monotonous and simple, the soul finds itself at ease, almost cradled in God's arms.

Another name for this way of praying is *breath prayer*. At times, this is the only prayer that works. This prayer does not come primarily from the mind, which is where most of our words come from; the breath prayer arises from the depths of our desire and need. In fact, it could more accurately be called a "gut prayer," because it comes from a deep gut level. This prayer is so simple that it requires no thought to remember it once we really know it is ours. It is so short (usually only six to eight syllables) that we can pray it rhythmically with the inhalation and exhalation of our breathing.

Breath prayer is powerful because it is an expression of our heart's deepest yearning coupled with the name for God that is most meaningful and intimate for us at this time. Usually our breath prayer will remain with us for quite some time, and we get to the point where it prays itself without our even having to think about it. Breath prayer does not replace other ways of praying; rather it is foundational to our whole prayer life, supporting it and making it possible for us to pray without ceasing. The breath prayer helps us to pray when we don't know how to pray. It gives us a way to pray even when we cannot pray formally. It can be used to usher us into times of contemplative prayer, and when our mind wanders, we can be brought back from distraction by simply repeating our breath prayer.

There is nothing magical or mystical about breath prayer. It is not the same thing as a mantra of Eastern meditation practice, nor is it the "heaping up of empty phrases" that Jesus warned against (Matthew 6:5). Rather, this prayer arises from deep within our being as a personal response to God at work within us. Breath prayer is to the spiritual life what oxygen and the pulmonary system are to life in the body, a way for us to breathe rhythmically and reflexively with the Spirit the very breath of God.

When you pray, do not try to express yourself in fancy words, for often it is the simple repetitious phrases of a little child that our Father in heaven finds most irresistible. Do not strive for verbosity lest your mind be distracted by a search for words. Single words by their very nature tend to concentrate the mind. When you find satisfaction in a certain word of your prayer, stop at that point.

JOHN CLIMACUS

✎ DISCOVERING YOUR BREATH PRAYER

You don't think your way into your breath prayer; you discover it by listening to your deepest longings and desires in God's presence. Sometimes our breath prayer will be a simple phrase that expresses the truest thing we know how to say to God at that time. At other times it may be a word or a phrase from a biblical prayer or a prayer of the church.

When I first started entering into silent prayer, it was all so new to me that the phrase "Here I am, Lord" was the simplest and truest way I could express my desire to be with God. These words really did capture the truth of my soul's longing at that time. More recent is the breath prayer I have already mentioned, the one that came during a time when I was aware (yet again!) of my need for deeper levels of transformation: "Lord Jesus Christ, have mercy on me, a sinner." The Jesus Prayer (as some call it) brings together what I know I need most these days—mercy—with the powerful name of Jesus Christ. This has been my breath prayer for several years now; it is the one that prays itself most naturally in me and connects me with something so deep inside that I honestly wouldn't know how else to access that place and bring it into God's presence.

The more I have prayed this prayer consciously, connecting it with my breathing, the more it has begun to pray itself in me before I have given it conscious thought. In moments of stress or fear, at times when sadness threatens to overwhelm me or awareness of my sin presses in, this prayer finds me, rather than my having to search for a way to pray. It grounds me in spiritual reality that is deeper than what is going on around me and keeps me from being swept away by my emotions or my circumstances. Furthermore, it connects me with spiritual seekers down through the ages, reaching all the way back to blind Bartimaeus, who have cried out to God from the deepest place within them.

The breath prayer is the prayer of the beggar and carries with it the intimacy of asking for what we need. To ask for what we really need is hard to do, but Scripture encourages us to make our requests known to God. Sometimes only desperation makes us willing to be that vulnerable. Praying the Jesus Prayer reminds me that I am not alone in these from-the-gut cries. It reminds me that to such cries Jesus responds with compassion and healing, and it gives me courage. This is a very different way of using words (or allowing God to use words) from what most of us are familiar with, but it connects us with God in the most intimate places of our lives and relieves us of the need to figure out how to pray.

🕮 PRAYER IN COMMUNITY

One of the most natural results of a developing a vibrant personal prayer life is that we begin to notice a deep desire to enter meaningfully into prayer in community with others. We long to experience Christ among us, to offer our worship, to confess our sins and receive assurance of God's forgiveness, and to seek his help for our own needs and the needs of others.

There are many ways of praying together with others. What has been most meaningful for me in recent years is the opportunity to pray with others at regular intervals throughout the day. In Christian tradition this is known as "praying the hours" or the Daily Office. I have had opportunities to pray this way most consistently with the communities of the Transforming Center, and it has anchored and shaped our lives and our work together in profound ways. Whether we are on retreat together, working together or even getting together socially, our steadiest commitment is to regularly turn our hearts toward God in prayer in ways that are appropriate to the part of the day we are in. In the morning we begin with praise, affirming God's presence with us and his loving care toward us and committing the work of the day to him. At midday, when tasks and to-do lists are pressing in and human effort is at its height, we stop to renew our awareness of God's presence, rest in him for a few moments and ask for his peace and guidance regarding the things that are concerning us. In the evening we place the cares of the day in God's hands and offer up general intercessions for ourselves and others, as well as bringing needs that are specific to us and burdens we are carrying for ourselves and others.

We are purposely not very wordy in our intercessions, because we realize that this is another place in the spiritual life where human striving and fixing can easily take over. As our own spiritual journey leads us to a greater capacity to be with God with what is true about us, to rest there and let him be in charge of what happens or what doesn't happen, so we are able to be with others and their needs quietly in God's presence as well. Intercessory prayer is not primarily about believing we know what someone else needs and then trying to tell God what the answer is. It is not about wrestling some result from God. Intercessory prayer is more about recognizing that we do not know how to pray for others—or ourselves for that matter—but the Holy Spirit knows. Since we understand that the Holy Spirit is already interceding for us before the throne of grace, we can bring a name or a need, express it simply and in the silence experience our own groaning and Holy Spirit's groaning for that person. We can listen for the prayer that is already being prayed for that person before the throne of grace, and without struggling hard to put things into words, we can enter into God's caring love for that person and wait with them and for them in God's presence. This is a wonderful way to release our burdens to God at the end of the workday.

When our community is together on retreat, we close the day with night prayer, confessing our sins, celebrating God's presence among us during the day and asking him to be with us as we rest. Our prayers are written in a liturgical format, so there is nothing to figure out. Scriptures are taken from the lectionary—a reading schedule that follows the Christian calendar—and are read without comment, giving God the opportunity to address us directly through his Word. The Gospel readings in particular help us to stay connected to the person of Christ as the model for our life and work.

In this way we give the Spirit of Christ access to us throughout the day as a community. We have been amazed at how the prayers and the Scriptures give us perspective, assurance and guidance according to our need, in ways that could not have been orchestrated by human planning. Many of us seek to pray the hours when we are alone as well, but we have discovered that a special power is released when two or three (or more!) gather in the presence of Christ and find ways to open their hearts to him together. It has been one of my deepest longings and my deepest joys to pray regularly with others who are also seeking God. Such prayer in community is profoundly life changing and worth any price one has to pay to find it!

⚬ ALL OF LIFE AS PRAYER

It has become increasingly difficult for me to distinguish prayer as a spiritual discipline from all the others. The longer I journey in the spiritual life, the more I experience all of life as prayer and the other disciplines as different ways of praying. Solitude and silence help me experience the more contemplative elements of prayer. *Lectio divina* is a way of praying the Scripture. Self-examination is the prayer in which I invite God to search me and reveal those things I need to know about myself. Discernment is the listening part of prayer: sitting with a question or decision in God's presence and waiting for the wisdom of God that is given as pure gift.

Any approach to the spiritual life that sets up false or awkward distinctions between prayer and life, or prayer and the other disciplines, seems to unnaturally rip apart elements of life that belong together or to unnecessarily complicate something that is in its essence quite simple. And so it happens that all of life becomes prayer. From prayers that are more formal and structured to those that are informal and spontaneous, from prayer with words to prayer that is beyond words, from the most intimate expressions of love expressed privately to God to words spoken in unison by God's people when they gather, from the eloquent written prayers of the church to the breath prayer that is nothing more than a gasp of need or a sigh of love or a groan of longing, from the prayers uttered in beautiful cathedrals to prayers offered on the side of a mountain—every breath we take can be a prayer, uniting our heart to God and harnessing the energy of our life to his great purposes.

May we ever be mere beginners in the life of prayer, always crying out, "Lord, teach us to pray."

〰 PRACTICE

There are several components to this practice so it could take one day or it could take a week. *Do not rush.* Take as long as you need to feel that your breath prayer really captures your heart's deepest need or desire at this time.

Begin by spending time quietly in God's presence, allowing yourself to settle into that beyond-words place of comfort and intimacy, receptivity and restful repose.

Then, imagine Jesus calling you by name and asking, "_____, what do you want?" It may help you to go back to your reflections on desire from chapter one. Allow your truest answer to this question to come up from your heart, and express this to God.

If it helps, you can begin by writing the following phrase in your journal and then just letting your response flow. "God, what I most want from you right now is . . ."

Work with the words or the phrase that comes until you feel that it captures your desire as truly as possible right now. This word or phrase will become the heart of your breath prayer.

Choose your favorite name or image for God as you are relating to him right now, such as God, Jesus, Father, Creator, Spirit, Breath of Life, Lord, Shepherd—whatever best captures your sense of who God is to you at this point in your relationship. "My most meaningful name for God is . . ."

Now combine your name for God with the expression of your heart's desire. Place it where it is easiest to say in the rhythm of your breathing.

If various possibilities come, write them down and eliminate or combine until you have a prayer of about six to eight syllables that flows smoothly when spoken aloud and captures the core of your deep yearning for wholeness and well-being in Christ. Your breath prayer could be a phrase from a biblical prayer or a Scripture passage. Just make sure it is short enough that it prays easily in the rhythm of your breathing.

Once you have chosen your breath prayer, pray it into the spaces of your day—when you are waiting, when you are worried and anxious, when you are needing some sense of God's presence. Over time, learn to pray it underneath all the other thoughts and words that swirl around you throughout your daily interactions. In times of solitude, pray this prayer as a way of entering into silence and of bringing your mind back to your desire when it begins to wander. Use the breath prayer God has given you consistently until you feel this prayer no longer captures your deepest need or desire or until God gives you another one.

5

HONORING THE BODY
Flesh-and-Blood Spirituality

The Christian practice of honoring the body is born of the confidence
that our bodies are made in the image of God's own goodness.
As the place where the divine presence dwells, our bodies are worthy
of care and blessing. . . . It is through our bodies that we participate
in God's activity in the world.

STEPHANIE PAULSELL

Surprisingly enough, it was in the process of staying faithful to the spiritual journey that I first began to face my profound ambivalence about life in a body. At the ripe old age of thirty, I could no longer ignore the fact that I was tired, lethargic and somewhat depressed. Thinking that my lethargy and lack of enthusiasm for life were psychological or spiritual problems, I went to a psychologist who was also a spiritual director. To my surprise, some of our initial conversations had to do with my physical condition: my eating patterns, how much sleep I was getting, whether I was getting any exercise, my water intake and my general attention to health issues. Even though over the years I had been intent on paying attention to the condition of my spiritual life, no one else had ever called any serious attention to the connection between my physical well-being and my life in Christ.

During that time I was reflecting on the story of Elijah's journey into

God's presence in 1 Kings 19, and I was struck by the attention God gave to Elijah's physical condition, going so far as to send an angel to guide him in caring for his body. I was comforted to find that even though Elijah was a great prophet, he had the same blind spot I was beginning to acknowledge in myself: he had let himself become so run down that God had to send an angel to strengthen his body before they could deal with anything else. The angel helped him pay attention to the condition of his body as the vehicle that would enable him to take the journey that lay ahead. The angel even pointed out that if he did not care for his body, the journey into the presence of God would be too much for him (1 Kings 19:7).

I, too, needed to face the fact that rather than caring for my body as I would any other highly valued gift, I had been using it for my own ends, to the point that it was now protesting. I hadn't been paying much attention to what I ate, so there was far too much sugar and junk food in my diet. Rather than getting enough rest, I had become quite dependent on caffeine for additional energy. I had never considered the importance of drinking enough water. And as a busy parent juggling the demands of home and family plus church and career, I thought that I didn't have enough time or energy to exercise or engage in physical activities that I enjoyed. Just as the angel gave Elijah very concrete instructions about eating, drinking and sleeping, I needed specific guidance for how to care for my body as a part of my spiritual practice and as preparation for the rigors of the spiritual journey into which I was being invited.

Up to this point, I had been quite out of touch with any sense that my life in a body had anything to do with my spirituality. Intent on trying to be "spiritual," I had somehow relegated life in the body to some lesser category that warranted very little of my attention. As long as no warning lights were flashing, I could ignore it in favor of other "more spiritual" endeavors such as silence and solitude, Scripture reflection, prayer, service and self-denial. The surrounding culture's idolization of perfect bodies and valuing of people according to their physical appearance and sexuality made me all the more hesitant to pay much attention to my body. I, for one, did not want to fall into the excesses of a secular culture that placed inordinate value on physical features rather than the beauty and dignity of the human soul as it reaches toward God.

Now I was confronting the reality that the physical and the spiritual are not as opposed to each other as I had thought. I was becoming more aware that I am not merely a soul and spirit; I am an embodied human being, and my body is the temple of the Holy Spirit (1 Corinthians 6:19). Whereas in Old Testament days the Holy Spirit came and went until eventually it found its dwelling place in a tabernacle constructed by human hands, God has chosen in these days to dwell permanently in the bodies of redeemed persons and in the body of Christ as it gathers. I had to grapple in very practical ways with the truth that in some unexplainable way God inhabits our bodies, making them a place where we can meet and know him. Beyond that, the Scriptures indicate that it is possible to *glorify God* in our bodies rather than merely glorifying the body, which seemed to be the focus of the surrounding culture. I grew more and more curious about what it might look like to glorify God in my body. I was pretty sure that walking around tired, overweight and overstimulated by sugar and caffeine was not it!

✆ RECEIVING THE GIFT OF LIFE IN THE BODY

Knowing that God has chosen to make our bodies his dwelling place opens the door to remarkable opportunities for heightening our awareness of God's presence. And isn't heightened awareness of God's presence with us and for us at all times, and our capacity to remain in vital connection with that presence, what the spiritual journey is all about?

Life in the body is, after all, a varied and wide-ranging experience, and some experiences are better than others. As I reflect on life in a body from a midlife vantage point, I can recall moments of gratitude for the particular body that was given to me and moments when I have wished mightily for a different one. There have been moments when touch was shared in loving ways and moments when touch was not so loving. There have been moments of keeping my body to myself and moments of deep sharing. There have been moments of strength and physical accomplishment as well as moments of physical weakness and vulnerability. Sometimes I do very well at living within the limits and bodily changes that accompany a particular life stage, and at other times I am resistant.

Only in recent years have I become more aware of the many good gifts given to us by way of life in a physical body. Prior to that, I guess I just took it all for granted. In addition, dualisms that are embedded in our religious traditions have create a false separation between the spiritual realm and the material world, leaving us "an ambiguous legacy" regarding the body. On the other hand, excessive and misdirected focus on the "perfect" body in secular culture, coupled with disturbing levels of irreverence regarding human sexuality, has made it all the more difficult to know how to relate to the body in a spiritual way.

These conflicting and ultimately unhelpful perspectives point to our need for learning how to receive the goodness of the body as part of our life in God that he pronounced good. We are in need of a sacramental approach to life, in which the body is understood to be sacred because it is the place where God's Spirit has chosen to dwell. Given this, *all* aspects of life in the body have the potential to become places where we meet and know God in unique ways.

All the great themes of Scripture affirm the significance of the body as a place where the presence of God can be known and experienced. The incarnation itself—Christ's choice to take on flesh and inhabit a human body—forever elevates the experience of embodiment to the heights of spiritual significance. Jesus, the supremely spiritual being who has existed for all eternity far beyond the physical, material world as we know it, chose to take the journey into human flesh and to become limited as we are by space and time. The central sacrament of our faith—the ritual and substance around which all Christians gather—is bread and wine that commemorates Jesus' life and death in a body made of flesh and blood. Even now, it is in these earthen vessels that the life of Christ continues to be made visible in our everyday lives. We carry within our body the treasure of the ministry that he has given us. Our bodies will be resurrected on the last day so that we can spend eternity not as disembodied spirits but as glorious embodied beings, worshiping in God's presence.

The spiritual discipline of honoring the body helps us find our way between the excesses of a culture that glorifies and objectifies the body and the excesses of Christian tradition that have often denigrated and ignored the body. As we become more intentional about finding this middle way, we will be surprised by the spontaneous combustion that comes when aspects of ourselves that were always meant to exist as an integrated whole finally come together in a way that produces great joy and vitality.

The appreciation of life in the body includes embracing our maleness or our femaleness, and thus our sexuality, as a gift from God that helps to reveal his true nature. None of us exists in this world apart from being one gender or another, and in fact our existence as male and female is one of the most complete ways God has revealed the diverse aspects of his own being. "God created humankind in his image; . . . male and female he created them" (Genesis 1:27). All of human experience is somehow connected, and all of it holds the possibility for abundant living, for the experience of grace and for the imprint of the divine. This means that our sexuality is a great gift, because it is a place we meet and know God in unique ways. False dualisms that separate our spirituality and our sexuality cut us off from knowing and experiencing God as One in whom there resides a powerful longing for union and oneness. Not only does such a dualistic approach cut us off from knowing God, it also cuts us off from knowing ourselves, embracing the powerful drives within us as a created good and bringing this essential part of ourselves into relationship with God.

As we begin to awaken fully to the spiritual, social and sexual dimensions of ourselves in God's presence, we find that they are inseparably intertwined and not to be compartmentalized. In fact, many spiritually awake people have noticed that

> our sexual feelings intensify as we are made whole. Many think that sexuality will go away or at least become more quiescent as we grow spiritually. On the contrary! As we abide more closely to the God who is the source of all creation, the God of the Incarnation, we begin to experience sexual energy in a new way, as a holy, inalienable generative force.

Learning to honor the body as a place where God makes his presence known becomes, then, an important discipline for the spiritual pilgrim.

CARING FOR THE BODY

My first forays into learning to honor my body had to do with simply learning how to care for it more intentionally. Through Elijah's story I realized that there is a very real connection between care for our body, our ability to continue deepening our relationship with God and our capacity to faithfully carry out God's purposes for our life over the long haul. I began to slowly shift my living patterns, eating better, drinking more water, getting more rest rather than resorting to the short-lived benefits of caffeine, and working my way slowly into a more active lifestyle that included walking, running and biking.

Some amazing changes started to take place. First of all, I began to have more energy and experienced a real lift in my spirits. I learned that one of God's gifts to us in the body is that exercise releases endorphins that are soothing to our emotions, ease pain and elevate our mood. Because I exercised outdoors, I began to experience those moments as times of significant connection with God through the expansiveness of the creation, the beauty of nature and my gratitude for the opportunity to enjoy life in a healthier body.

Also, some of my spiritual practices began to coincide quite naturally with my physical disciplines. Times of running and walking became moments of turning my heart toward God. Because nighttime has been the best and most consistent time for me to walk and jog, I found myself naturally using those times to engage in the examen of consciousness and conscience. While my body was occupied with physical activity, my heart and mind were freed up to reflect on my day and invite God to help me notice those times when the Spirit was at work guiding, protecting, comforting me. Somehow the privacy afforded by the darkness and the expansiveness of the night sky created a setting that was quiet and safe enough for me to allow God to help me see those times when I had fallen short of love that day, to confess sin, to release the day's burdens and look toward a new day with hope and fresh resolve.

For years now I have used a daily bike ride to a nearby retreat center as a way of connecting physical exercise with time for silence and prayer. This is as much a spiritual practice for me as sitting at home with my Bible open, because it connects every part of me with the One who created me. I now understand that the exhilaration I experience in these moments comes from the connection between physical and the spiritual that is a part of the goodness that God built into creation.

Interestingly enough, even secular research indicates that exercise and spirituality go hand in hand. "A biological mechanism is at work," says William C. Bushell, a Massachusetts Institute of Technology research scientist specializing in medicine and anthropology. "Whatever creator made the body had this in mind. It comes out in physiological science like a clear blueprint." Exercise brings mental and physiological changes, including the flood of body-made opiates that induce what's called the "runner's high." This physiological dynamic can create a change in consciousness, a kind of expansiveness in which the runner feels more integrated with his or her surroundings and the Creator himself.

Your opportunities to link your physical activity with your spiritual practices may be very different from mine, depending on the activities you enjoy and your physical capacities. The point here is that spiritual disciplines do not all have to be practiced while one sits quiet and still. There are many creative ways to forge a life-giving connection between our spiritual life and life in our body; the key is our intent and our attention to the way in which God makes himself known in this most basic aspect of our existence.

LISTENING TO THE BODY

Our bodies have much to tell us if we could only figure out how to listen. In fact, oftentimes God speaks to us through our body. Most times, our body is the first to know if we are overcommitted, stressed, uneasy or joyful, and when we need to attend to something that is causing us pain or disease.

Elouise Renich Fraser, in her book *Confessions of a Beginning Theologian,* writes about the significant role that listening to her body has played in her personal and theological journey.

> My body, once ignored and despised, has become an ally in the reorientation of my internal and external life. It lets me know when I'm running away, avoiding yet another of God's invitations to look into my past and the way it binds me as a theologian. I can't trust my mind as often as I trust my body. My mind tries to talk me into business as usual, but my body isn't fooled. Insomnia, intestinal pain and diarrhea let me know there's work to be done.

Paying attention to what we are experiencing in our body can open up windows of insight that might not otherwise be opened. For instance, the experience of consolation and desolation, explored earlier, is in many ways a bodily experience. A flow of energy into us, or its draining away from us, can be felt in our body if we are in touch with it. Remember God's assurances to the people of Israel that the ability to choose life and follow God was not to be found in some faraway place. "No, the word [of God] is very near to you; it is in your mouth and in your heart for you to observe" (Deuteronomy 30:14). In other words, what you need to know to be well is already known in your body if you will just pay attention.

One area of my life where this has really proved to be true is my work and vocation. As I have worked to clarify my calling, I have learned to pay attention to my energy levels in response to different activities. If I experience a particular activity as being inordinately draining, I begin to consider very carefully how much of myself God wants me to give to that. On the other hand, if I feel particularly energized by a certain person or activity, I can pay attention to how God may be leading me to incorporate more of that into my life.

Paying attention to what gives our body and our spirit a sense of life or drains life from us can help us stay connected with God's guiding presence. When I honor my body by "listening" to tension, discomfort, lightness, or joy and wonder, asking, *Now what is that about?* often God speaks into that awareness with truth and insight that proves very helpful over the long haul.

⚕ PRAYING IN THE BODY

While we might think of prayer as an activity that engages us primarily on a soul level, the Scriptures tell us plainly that the body is a temple of the Holy Spirit, and a temple, after all, is a place of prayer and worship. Prayer, as discussed earlier, is primarily about deepening our intimacy with God. Human desire for God is experienced in the flesh as a visceral longing, a hunger and a thirst. "O God, you are my God, I seek you, my soul thirsts for you, my flesh faints for you" (Psalm 63:1).

Intimacy happens as we bring more and more of ourselves into God's presence. To pray with soul *and* body means, says Jane Vennard, "praying with all of who we are: our physicality, our emotions, our intuitions, our imaginations, our minds and all of our experiences. Therefore when we pray with body and soul, or love with body and soul, or belong with body and soul, we are believing, responding, surrendering with all of who we are."

When we pray, our posture and our bodily position can be an important aspect of our communication with God. To settle into a relaxed and comfortable position, letting go, allowing a chair to fully support your body, breathing deeply in a way that releases tension, can be a very tangible way of telling God that we are bringing our whole self into his presence—body, mind and spirit. With our body we are telling God that we trust him and rest in him and are available to him.

Have you ever been in a worship service and noticed your body's desire to kneel down? Have you ever felt so humbled in God's presence that you wanted to lie flat on your face? Have you ever longed to curl up and be held by God? Any of these sensations can be your body telling you how it wants or needs to pray and can serve as a guide for you in your praying. Kneeling or even lying prostrate on the floor can give physical expression to the posture of our heart or lead us into a more prayerful, humble stance before God. Praying with our hands open can be a way of expressing our openness to God and our willingness to receive whatever he wants to give. When words become inadequate to express our joy and praise, we pray with our body by lifting our hands or moving or dancing.

Walking meditation is also a powerful way of connecting with God. There are several ways to meditate while walking, but the simplest is to take a slow, "sensing" walk in which the express purpose is to be with God and consciously commune with him through the physical senses. I remember the first time I took a hike in the woods for the express purpose of paying attention to manifestations of God through nature. The warmth of the sun felt like God's presence warming me. There was a whole world of bugs and plants and rocks and trees and streams and animals that were blissfully unaware of the things that seemed so big in my life; all of a sudden many things that had seemed all-important shrank to a more appropriate size in my heart. As I sat on a tree trunk that had fallen across a stream, I prayed and felt myself rejuvenated by the beauty and the silence. I saw hundreds of tadpoles swimming around in a puddle that had formed in a rut—of all things!—and it reminded me that life can spring up anywhere, even in the dry and rutted places of my own life. I paid attention to how good it felt to be in my body, climbed a hill until my heart beat fast, got sweaty and lay down exhausted when I got back—full of a sense of the immensity and yet the nearness of God.

If that's not prayer, I don't know what is!

PRACTICING WHOLENESS

God has created us for wholeness. When aspects of ourselves that were always meant to exist together are reintegrated, the result is a combustion of joy and vitality that goes far beyond the physical dimension. It is a spiritual vitality that speaks volumes about the abundance of our life in Christ. Moments of physical activity and exercise can become prayers of gratitude and moments of consecration. Eating food that we enjoy and is healthful for us can be the occasion of experiencing God's care for us, reminding us of our dependency on him and of his faithfulness to care for our needs. By scheduling at least some of our meals at times when we can eat slowly and prayerfully, we can make mealtimes occasions of true communion and gratitude. Paying more attention to the act of bathing or showering can heighten our awareness of our human vulnerability and also the wonder and beauty of our body. By fully receiving the loving touch of friends and family members, we allow God to minister to our very human needs for love and meaningful connection. When we give ourselves wholeheartedly to the sexual experience with our spouse or learn how to embrace our sexuality in periods of singleness, we say a profound yes to God's call to live in this world as human beings created male and female.

These days my most profound moments of joy, comfort and connection with God seem to come most regularly in the context of bodily experience. My late-night jogs are prayers of gratitude in which no words are needed. As I care for my body more wisely, I am conscious of a life-giving energy that is always being renewed as a gift from my amazing Creator God. And as I have learned to listen to my body, I have grown in the capacity to discern God's guidance and trust it, even in the midst of great complexity. Every day I am discovering in fresh ways that life lived fully in the body *is* the truly spiritual life.

✸ PRACTICE

Paying attention to your breathing is one of the simplest ways of getting in touch with your existence as a body. Settle into a comfortable position, either in a chair or on the floor, and pay attention to your breathing. Notice if your breathing is shallow, and take time to breathe deeply. Allow your breathing to release any tension you are holding in your back, your shoulders, your arms. Adjust your body for greater comfort, and allow yourself to relax into your chair or cushion as a physical expression of your trust in God.

Gently turn your attention to your body, and invite God to speak to you through your body. First of all, just notice how you feel about life in your body. Are you embarrassed about it? Do you enjoy it? What happens inside you when you consider the idea of honoring your body or meeting God in your body?

What is the condition of your body these days? Have you been caring for it consistently—eating right, sleeping enough, exercising, attending to medical issues and concerns—or have you been ignoring it or even abusing it in some way? Sit with your awareness and talk to God about it. Listen for his response.

Is there anything your body is trying to tell you? Any place of tension or discomfort that you have been ignoring? Any medical issue that requires attention? Any feeling of dis-ease that is vaguely unsettling and seems to persist? Listen to see if there is anything you have been keeping outside your awareness, and let it come fully into your awareness in God's presence.

Is there any way your body wants to pray right now? Any way you could express yourself to God physically? Go ahead, follow your body's lead, and pray with your body and soul.

In your solitude times, begin with a few moments for breathing and settling into your body. Notice if any of your spiritual practices might have some connection with physical activities that you enjoy. Notice how you experience God's presence through a greater appreciation for life in your body.

6

SELF-EXAMINATION

Bringing My Whole Self Before God

*Many avoid the path of self-knowledge because they are afraid of
being swallowed up in their own abysses. But Christians have
confidence that Christ has lived through all the abysses of human life
and that he goes with us when we dare to engage in sincere
confrontation with ourselves. Because God loves us
unconditionally—along with our dark sides—we don't need to
dodge ourselves. In the light of this love the pain of self-knowledge can
be at the same time the beginning of our healing.*

ANDREAS EBERT

There comes a time in the spiritual life when one of the major things
God is up to is to lovingly help us see ourselves more clearly. This is a
most challenging element of the spiritual life, one that most of us shrink
from with more than a little bit of dread. Some of us have been so shaped
by shame-based family or church systems that we resist entering into
deeper levels of self-knowledge for fear of feeling debilitated by shame or
swept away by remorse. For others, our sense of worth is so fragile or our
perfectionism so pronounced that we are not sure we could bear facing
the truth of our own darkness without becoming completely unraveled.

And yet one of the deepest longings of the human heart is to be
known and loved unconditionally. We long to know that someone in this

world knows everything about us and loves us anyway. Beyond the surface affirmations that come through our achievements and social contacts, we long to be seen and celebrated for that which is deeply good and worthwhile in us, *and* we long for a love that is strong enough to contain our frailty and sinfulness. Something in us knows that such love is a transforming power.

The problem is that most of us aren't willing to take the risk of being seen so completely. There is always something we're hiding for fear that we will be rejected in the end. We may have gotten close to the possibility of this kind of love at one time or another, but we haven't known how to let it penetrate our defenses so that we can receive it. All of us would prefer to have the experience of unconditional love without having to take the risk of letting someone know us that well!

The desire and the need for unconditional love are heightened as we become more aware of those places where we are not like Christ—an inevitability of the spiritual journey. As we become more spiritually attuned, we become painfully aware of how negative thought patterns and relating patterns hurt ourselves and others. We see the places where we are incapable of love and true self-giving. We realize that our responses to wounds we've received have caused us to become hard and self-protective. We notice the subtleties of our jealousies, our mean-spiritedness, our manipulations, our controlling ways, and our mistrust of God and others that keeps us from giving ourselves wholeheartedly. Having tried every self-help approach we know, we are devastated to admit that real, fundamental change is beyond our reach. The heart cries out to be free from its bondage.

Eventually we discover that, as painful as it is, this waking up to what is real is where the action is, spiritually speaking. As Robert Mulholland says: "Our cross is the point of our unlikeness to the image of Christ, where we must die to self in order to be raised to God into the wholeness of life in the image of Christ. . . . So the process of being conformed to the image of Christ takes place *right there at that point* of our unlikeness to Christ."

But even knowing this, we vacillate between our tendency to hide that which is truest about us and our longing to be changed by love. We are drawn to the possibility of deeper freedom and spiritual transformation, yet we would like to avoid the full weight of what that might require of us. We need a practice that offers us a way of opening to the love of God in the places of our brokenness and sin—which is the only way true spiritual transformation ever takes place.

WAKING UP TO THE PRESENCE OF GOD

Self-examination is a practice that facilitates spiritual awakening—an awakening to the presence of God as God really is and an awakening to ourselves as we really are. When practiced rightly, it leads us into a greater sense of God's constant loving presence in our life, it fosters a celebration of our created self, it offers us a safe place to see and name those places where we are not like Christ, and it opens us up to deeper levels of spiritual transformation. Self-examination is the Christian practice that opens us to the love we seek.

Psalm 139:23-24 is perhaps the most familiar passage articulating the soul's invitation to God to guide the self-examination process: "Search me, O God, and know my heart; test me and know my thoughts. See if there is any wicked way in me, and lead me in the way everlasting." A full exploration of Psalm 139, however, offers us a more complete and balanced approach to self-examination. It begins with God.

The psalm begins by acknowledging that God has *already* searched me and already knows me through and through! He knows the intimacies and the intricacies of my inner world—my thoughts and feelings— as well as my comings and goings in the outer world. And the good news is that there is nothing I can do, nothing that God knows about me, and no place I can go where I am beyond his presence. Entering fully into the self-examination process begins with knowing that I am forever secure in God's love.

> O LORD, you have searched me and known me.
> You know when I sit down and when I rise up;
> > you discern my thoughts from far away.
> You search out my path and my lying down,
> > and are acquainted with all of my ways.
> Even before a word is on my tongue,
> > O LORD, you know it completely. (verses 1-4)

There is a paradox, of course, in the truth that I am inviting God to search me and know me when in fact he already has searched me and known me. This may point to the fact that the real issue in self-examination is not that I am inviting God to know me (since he already does) but that I am inviting God to help *me* know me. This is clearly the bigger challenge anyway, since we all have such finely tuned tactics for protecting ourselves from knowing what we don't want to know. Like a small child who "hides" by covering her eyes, thinking that if she can't see you, you can't see her, we think that if we don't acknowledge what is true about us, maybe God won't notice it either!

Basically the experience of being known so intimately—of having God "hem me in behind and before" (verse 5)—is one I welcome; it feels like being held securely and safely. But there are

While the truth that we cannot escape God's all-seeing eye may weigh us down at times, it is finally the only remedy for our uneasiness. If we wish to hide from the penetrating gaze of holy love, it is because we know it falls on what is unholy and unloving within us. Only under God's steady gaze of love are we able to find the healing and restoration we so desperately need.

MARJORIE THOMPSON,
SOULFEAST

other times when the experience of having God "hem me in" feels, well, a little bit stifling. I'm not sure I like being known that well or having someone come in so close. A little privacy, please! But as I become more and more aware of God's presence, I discover that the experience for which my soul has longed—to have someone know everything about me and love me anyway—is here for me now. That love becomes a safe harbor within which I am able to know and be known.

⚮ THE EXAMEN OF CONSCIOUSNESS

It takes time and practice to recognize the unconditional love and presence of God as the ultimate and unchanging reality of our life. One way to develop our capacities to recognize the presence of God is to engage in what is identified in ancient tradition as the *examen of consciousness,* or what we might call a daily review. This is a simple discipline that helps us to become more God conscious, heightening our awareness that God is indeed with us when we lie down to sleep, when we wake up and in every moment in between. We discover that we really are being led by the hand of God. Even when things seem dark, a light comes from God that can illuminate the deepest darkness.

The examen of consciousness involves taking a few moments at the end of each day to go back over the events of the day and invite God to show us where he was present with us and how we responded to his presence. We might ask ourselves, *How was God present with me today? What promptings did I notice? How did I respond or not respond?*

When we first begin practicing this discipline, we may not be conscious of God's presence at all during the moments of the day, but our examen helps us to become conscious of evidence we might not otherwise have noticed. As we reflect prayerfully on the day, we may realize that someone was particularly kind or compassionate toward us and that God was loving us through that person. Or perhaps there was a moment when we narrowly escaped harm or injury, and as we look back, we see more clearly that God was there protecting us. We may also notice something as seemingly inconsequential as the choice to hold our tongue rather than say something critical or gossipy, or a moment when we were able to be loving and selfless in a situation where usually we would have been self-serving or mean. And we know that the ability to do so came from God at work in our life.

As we review our days in this manner, we will notice times and places where we got a glimpse of God-with-us but failed to respond. Perhaps we were moving too fast to really notice, or we were stubborn or lazy or felt it would require too much of us. Observing such a missed opportunity might fill us with regret, but this honing of our awareness opens up the opportunity for us to make a different choice next time. Through the examen of consciousness, we become aware of God's presence with us even in moments that are tinged with regret, and we begin to believe, little by little, that nothing can take us out of God's presence. Through faithful practice of this discipline we begin to discover, as the psalmist did, that even those places within us that feel very dark and uninhabitable are places where God's presence is real.

> Where can I go from your spirit?
> > Or where can I flee from your presence? . . .
> Even the darkness is not dark to you;
> > the night is as bright as the day,
> > for darkness is as light to you. (verses 7, 12)

✕ AWAKENING TO THE GIFT OF YOUR CREATED SELF

The second section of this psalm (verses 13-18) points to the fact that healthy self-examination includes receiving and celebrating the goodness of who we are as created beings. A balanced approach to spiritual transformation involves joyful acceptance of who we are as one of God's greatest gifts to ourselves and to others. This goodness includes the uniqueness of our body, our personality, the configuration of our soul and its unique way of relating to God, our background and experience, even those things that we might consider to be liabilities or deformities.

> For it was you who formed my inward parts;
>> you knit me together in my mother's womb.
> I praise you, for I am fearfully and wonderfully made. (verses 13-14)

When was the last time you celebrated yourself as David celebrates himself here? When was the last time you looked at your body and thought it was beautiful or strong or amazing? When was the last time you experienced some aspect of life in your body—running, walking, dancing, lovemaking, rock climbing, birthing a baby, painting—and thought, *It is the most wonderful thing that I am able to do this*? When was the last time you celebrated some unusual dimension of your personality or some expression of your soul and thought, *There are many things that I do, but this is who I am! I love being this person God has made me to be*?

It may seem like a simple thing, but for many it is not. Some of us have deep feelings of ambivalence or even shame about some part of our body, or we feel disconnected and uncomfortable with life in a body in general. For others some aspect of the personality or some element of the soul is deeply embarrassing, and we have not yet come to a place where we can celebrate that in the light of God's presence.

In my early thirties I took a personality test as part of my job on a church staff team. The exercise was designed to help us get to know ourselves and each other better in order to increase team effectiveness, but it had quite a different effect on me! This particular test used the letters DISC to indicate four personality traits—Dominant, Inspiring, Steady, Compliant. While none of the categories were particularly exciting to me, I was most embarrassed to have the test result indicate that I was a high D (dominant). Believe me, this was not a compliment. No woman in my circles at that time wanted to be identified this way! The only sav-

ing grace was that no one else on the team guessed that I was a high D;
they thought I was a high I (influencing, inspirational)—which, of
course, meant I had done a good job of hiding my real self. Needless to
say, I was far from being able to celebrate my created self.

My father has endured similar struggles. Raised in a blue-collar town
in southern Illinois, he felt isolated; the part of him that is a poet and a
mystic, deeply responsive to beauty and art, was hardly understood by
the people around him, let alone celebrated or cultivated. Later on, as an
itinerant preacher in fundamentalist Christian circles with stripped-
down church buildings and minimal use of a piano in worship, he still
found no place for embracing these essential elements of his soul. For
many years he tried hard to repress those aspects of himself that couldn't
find expression in our cultural milieu, but it was a source of sadness and
depression. Only recently has he embraced these parts of himself more
freely—spending hours and hours at art museums, attending concerts,
visiting cathedrals, choosing church services that incorporate great music and fine art. He is letting these parts of himself live and breathe rather
than trying to keep them hidden. His ability to receive his created self as
the gift it is has been a blessing not only to him but also to his children,
each of whom embody different aspects of who he is.

How many people do you know who are effective at being themselves
and letting God use that? This psalm invites us to do just that—to become
really effective at being ourselves and letting God use that for his glory.

WAKING UP TO THE DARKNESS WITHIN

For the longest time I have pondered the next verses in Psalm 139,
verses 19-22, wondering what place such expressions of hatred and
loathing have in the midst of such a beautiful psalm.

> O that you would kill the wicked, O God,
>   and that the bloodthirsty would depart from me—

those who speak of you maliciously,
>and lift themselves up against you for evil!
Do I not hate those who hate you, O LORD?
>And do I not loathe those who rise up against you?
I hate them with perfect hatred;
>I count them my enemies.

I know from my Bible college and seminary days that this is an *imprecatory* psalm, in which David expresses emotions of righteous anger and hatred toward God's enemies in ways that were common for God-fearing Jews. But it is all too easy to dismiss these verses by relegating them to some preconceived category. If we focus solely on the literary genre these verses fit into, we run the risk of missing the point. David was a man in the process of spiritual transformation. Throughout the Psalms he is seen crying out for deeper levels of intimacy with God and the transformation that it would bring about in his own life—the very things many of us are seeking. Perhaps more than any other biblical character, David (through his writing) allows us a window into the inner workings of the human soul. By looking through the window of David's life, we get glimpses of how it is that people draw closer to God and how they grow and change. More than any other character in the Bible, David's life illustrates the self-examination process—the movement from total lack of awareness to self-awareness, confession of sin, forgiveness, cleansing and real life change.

If we look at these verses to discover what is happening in the process of his spiritual transformation, it is clear that David is now entering into the heart of the self-examination process. In the safety that comes from knowing that he is secure in God and has been lovingly formed by God, he is able to let the darker elements of himself emerge in God's presence. The confidence he expressed earlier in the psalm about finding God's presence in the dark places and about how the light of God can penetrate even the darkest night is crucial, for it applies not only to the darkness of geographical places but, even more important, to the dark places within the human soul.

In addition, David's certainty that the person God created him to be is deeply good has become the bedrock of his identity; he is able to let the parts that are confusing even to himself come into the light of God's presence so that God can show him what is good and what is evil. His basic identity is so secure that he is able to risk allowing all facets of himself to be seen without fear of God's abandoning him or fear of losing his sense of himself. In a rush of self-disclosure, he pours out his truest thoughts and feelings and then invites God to help him sort it all out. Whether these are feelings that all devout Jews feel or not and whether they are justifiable to others or not, David is saying "I really don't know what is good and what is evil within me."

> Search me, oh God, and know my heart;
>> test me and know my thoughts.
> See if there is any wicked way in me,
>> and lead me in the way everlasting. (verses 23-24)

Many of us cannot even register the kind of relational safety that enabled David to be so free with himself in God's presence. Human beings' abandoning each other is such a norm in contemporary relationships that while in our head we can acknowledge the possibility of such love and faithfulness, little in our experience indicates that complete love and safety really do exist for us. All of us have had normal experiences of abandonment—a best friend in childhood deciding they don't like us anymore, a high school romance coming to an end. But there are deeper abandonments that have the capacity to embed themselves so deep inside us that they shape our ability to trust ourselves to the love of God, particularly when it comes to self-examination in God's presence. Perhaps our mother or father withdrew into silence when we were bad, and we thus experienced love as a very conditional thing. Or one of our parents divorced the other and left the family, which caused us, in our childlike way, to wonder if some fundamental flaw or unlovable quality in us caused them to abandon us. Or later on, perhaps we had a spouse who walked out of the marriage because of some perceived flaw. Or there was a job to which we gave our best and then we were let go unexpectedly.

No matter what we believe with our head, such experiences shape us from the inside and determine what we know experientially. If we harbor any concern that we might be abandoned because of some lack in ourselves or some untrustworthiness in the other, it will be very difficult to give ourselves to God's penetrating gaze. However, when we have come to a place of certainty in the steadfastness of God's love and are anchored by a sense of the basic goodness of our created self, there is nothing to lose and everything to gain in inviting God to search us and know us to our very depths. *Even the darkness is not dark to you.*

EXAMEN OF CONSCIENCE

The move from seeing God more clearly (examen of consciouness) to seeing *ourselves* more clearly in the light of God's presence is a natural one. We call this the examen of conscience. It is similar to the examen of consciousness in that it involves reviewing your day or your week, only this time asking God to bring to mind attitudes, actions and moments when you fell short of exhibiting the character of Christ or the fruit of the Spirit. When we enter into the examen of conscience, we are willing to listen without defending and to see without rationalizing. We do not depend on our own morbid introspections or keen insights; rather, we surrender ourselves to the Spirit of God, who reveals truth to us as we are able to bear it. As God brings different areas to mind, we are willing to reflect on what contributed to the situation and how we might respond differently in the future. It is the willingness to allow God to guide the process that elevates it from a self-help project to a spiritual practice.

The examen of conscience involves three elements that are subtle and yet distinct. Sometimes all three take place at once, but other times it is more of a process. The first element is simply *seeing* something that went wrong in a behavior or an action. It might be a vague sense of something that wasn't quite right (for instance, a subtle resistance to doing something loving for another person), or it could be a wrong that was more clear-cut (such as an angry outburst). We start to have some awareness of what happened, and we may get a glimpse of how our action or lack of action has fallen short of Christlikeness and/or how it has wounded others. The next move is being willing to name our failure for what it is and also to name what was going on inside us, seeking some understanding of the inner dynamics that caused the behavior. In this element of the process we really do need God to guide us, because often our inner wounds, character deficiencies and sin patterns are unknown to us and we need God to reveal them. The final move is confession.

Awakening to our sin initiates a stage in the spiritual life classically understood as *purgation,* in which God gradually strips us of more and more layers of our own sinfulness. Robert Mullholland helpfully distinguishes these various layers. First of all there is the renunciation of all blatant inconsistencies with wholeness in Christ—obvious sins like those that Paul lists in passages like Galatians 5:19-21, which even our culture eschews. Then purgation moves to other deliberate sins that may be "normal" and "acceptable" in our culture but are clearly not acceptable in God's economy—for instance, sexual sin. There may also be behaviors that are not inherently bad but would be unloving or unhelpful in a particular context, like the eating of meat in Paul's day (see Romans 14).

Next, purgation causes us to become aware of unconscious sins and omissions; these are problems we might not have noticed earlier on, but now we see them as being hindrances to our growth. We might begin see how we are driven in subtle ways by our ego, how we subtly manipulate others to get our own way or how we do not always tell the truth. It is painful to see and name such twisted dynamics within us, and perhaps we are embarrassed that we did not see them before. Yet this is a necessary part of bringing our whole self into God's presence.

The final stage in the purgation process deals with the deep-seated attitudes and inner orientations out of which our behavior patterns flow. Here God is dealing primarily with our "trust structures," especially those deep postures of our being that do not rely on God but on self for our well-being. Here we make the devastating discovery of all the ways in which we are captive to our own anxieties, driven by our need to control God and others and impose our own order on things. We begin to get a glimpse of the false self that functions primarily to keep us safe rather than helping us to know how to abandon ourselves to God. At this level, we must take a hard look: are we really trusting ourselves to God and to the flow of God's Spirit, or are we bound up by defensive, self-protective patterns that serve only to help us maintain our fragile sense of security and well-being in the world?

As painful as it is to have these layers of the false self stripped away, it is really evidence of God's grace. It is evidence that God is at work, leading us out of bondage to sin into the freedom for love that is ours in Christ. At every level of the purgation process we are led toward the final and most transforming aspect of the self-examination process, which is confession, the discipline that results in our ultimate freedom.

THE FREEDOM OF CONFESSION

Confession is the endgame in the self-examination process, but it is the part we shrink from the most. Confession requires the willingness to acknowledge and take responsibility not only for the outward manifestations of our sin but also for the inner dynamics that produced the sinful or negative behaviors. Confession requires us to say our failure out loud to ourselves, to God and to the person(s) we have hurt and to take steps to renounce it for Christ's sake, even making restitution if that is needed.

There is a big difference between saying, "I'm sorry *if* I hurt you," and saying, "I'm sorry I hurt you. I realize now that it was my insecurity that produced such bad behavior. I have really prayed about this, and I believe God is showing me how I can avoid doing that again. Will you forgive me?" Confession at this level is so countercultural for so many reasons that it is hard to know how to begin to talk about it; however, to stop short of confession is to stop short of the deepest levels of transformation.

Many of us lack positive models and processes for understanding how a person sees, names and takes personal responsibility for who they are and how they behave. In many families no one takes responsibility for their actions; when something goes wrong, the blame gets passed from person to person until it lands (usually) with the most defenseless person in the system. I have talked to young people who have never heard a parent or any adult actually admit to sin or bad behavior or offer an apology without making excuses or blaming someone else.

In addition, our culture promotes a profound sense of denial about the presence of sin in our lives and the ways our sins and negative patterns wound others. In our litigious milieu, even when something is our fault, we are encouraged not to admit it unless we can derive some benefit from that. We are, in fact, encouraged to twist facts or misuse language such that the spotlight of blame can be focused somewhere else. We use all sorts of means, ranging from flat-out denial to subtle misuse of language, to avoid having to admit when we are wrong.

One church leader dealt with a parishioner in a way that was mean and even slanderous. When confronted with such blatantly bad behavior, the best this leader could do was to acknowledge that her communication was "less than artful." Such a weak admission showed little capacity for true self-awareness, self-examination and confession. How healing it would have been if this leader could have acknowledged how her behavior had wounded another, reflected a bit on what was happening inside her that led her to make such cutting remarks, offered a sincere apology and asked for forgiveness. But alas, these patterns do not come naturally for us as individuals or as a culture.

Confession, when practiced fully, is personal (between me and God), interpersonal (with a trusted friend or confessor, with the person I have hurt or offended) and corporate (in the context of worship in community). The interplay among these three keeps confession healthy and productive. One disturbing tendency among Christians is that it is all too easy for us to confess our sins to God privately or to make a general confession as part of a church service; it is much harder to confess our selfishness directly to our spouse, our jealousy to a friend, our impatience to our children or our ego-driven pushing to our colleagues. How is it that we can enter into confession in a church service but have such a hard time naming and confessing our sin face to face in the moment with someone we have hurt or offended? "I'm sorry my jealousy kept me from joining you in celebrating your success." "I'm sorry that my idealism kept me pushing my agenda rather than being able to accept what is real." "I'm sorry that my out-of-control schedule has kept me so self-absorbed and distant that I wasn't able to be there for you during that difficult time." One thing we can know for sure is that when we are confessing our sin to God but not to the people around us in ordinary, nitty-gritty life, there is not much real spiritual transformation going on.

AWAKENING TO GOD'S FORGIVENESS

Confession is good for the soul. It is good for the soul because it opens us to the experience of being forgiven and the freedom that comes on the other side. When the process is complete, self-examination and confession result in an appropriate lightness about our sin and a sense of unburdening. While the "godly grief that leads to repentance" (2 Corinthians 7:10) is part of the process and may be very deep as we see ourselves for who we are, confession does not ultimately lead us to shame or obsession but rather to a sense of cleansing and release. "For you shall know the truth, and the truth shall set you free" (John 8:32).

One of the most beautiful experiences of this awakening that I have witnessed was with our oldest 'daughter, Charity, when she was just fifteen years old. (She has given her permission for me to tell this story.) Chris and I had been away for the evening celebrating a friend's birthday, and when we came home, things didn't feel right in the house. The kitchen floor and counters looked clean, but they were a bit sticky; there was trash in the trash cans from food items that we don't use, and Charity was acting a bit strange. We probed, but she kept assuring us that everything was fine.

The next day I continued to feel disturbed, certain that something had gone on in our house while we were gone. I told Charity that if she didn't tell us what had happened, I would have to call the police because I felt that someone had been in our house. At that point she admitted that there had been people in the house and there had been some drinking, but the details were very fuzzy and changed with each telling. She was clearly not telling us the whole story.

This happened on a Friday night. By Sunday we were able to piece together who had been at the house that evening, but we still were not getting to the truth. I told Charity that I was going to call the parents of each young person who had been there and tell them that there had been a drinking party at our house, and to get to the bottom of it, we would like the parents to come to our house with their child the following evening so that we could talk about it. As you can imagine, Charity was scared to death and had no idea what to expect. We assured her that our intent was to be loving but that we had a right to know what had gone on in our house, the parents had a right to know what their kids were up to, the young people needed a chance to take responsibility for their actions, and we parents needed a chance to say that we loved them too much to let this kind of thing go on without dealing with it.

By the time Monday evening came, Charity had told us the whole truth, and one of the neighbors had let us know that he'd had to drive one young man home because he was too drunk to drive. But we still felt that the parents needed to be informed, and the young people needed an opportunity to take responsibility for their actions. So we continued with our plans for a meeting. To our surprise, all the parents came (not just one but both parents!) along with their children; about thirty of us gathered in our living room to let the truth be told.

With no place to hide, each young person had to take responsibility for their part of what happened. Charity had invited a few close friends over while we weren't there (which she was not allowed to do). When other teens (including some older ones who could drive) found out that there were no parents at home, they came over with liquor, and she let them in. One young man confessed that in his backpack he had brought a bottle of vodka that he had taken from his girlfriend's grandparents' home. Another confessed to taking his mother's car out of the garage without her knowledge to go buy beer. Another confessed to having had so much to drink that he couldn't stop vomiting (thus the sticky counters). The young man whom our neighbors had to drive home confessed that he had been too drunk to drive. It was a shocking and sobering evening.

Once the whole story had been told to everyone's satisfaction and the parents had had time to ask all their questions, Charity made her own confession. Though she could have fudged a bit and blamed the problems on those who brought the liquor, she took full responsibility for her actions. With tears and brokenness she confessed to her friends and their parents, "The fact that this happened is my fault. If I had not had people over when I wasn't supposed to, this would not have happened. If I had not opened the door and let everyone in, this would not have happened. If I had called someone to help, this would not have happened. I am sorry. The thing that hurts me most is the thought that you might not trust me anymore. I hope that you can forgive me and that you will trust me again to be a good friend to your son or daughter." By this time almost everyone was crying.

When it was over, there were hugs all around and a deep sense of gratitude for what had taken place. The young people were grateful for the love that had been shown to them (strange as it may seem), and the parents were grateful that someone had cared enough to provide a way for them to know what was happening in their children's lives. Many of the parents hugged Charity and told her that they loved her and did forgive her.

After everyone had left, we sat quietly together, reflecting on the love that had been shown, and Charity made a statement I will never forget. Her eyes were shining with a brightness and a peace I had never seen in her before, and she said, "I don't care what happens to me now. Now I know I am forgiven."

✺ PRACTICE

This is a practice that incorporates all of the elements of self-examination that we have explored in this chapter: examen of consciousness, examen of conscience and confession. While the steps may seem a bit ponderous as laid out here, once you become accustomed to them, they become less linear and you can give yourself to the underlying rhythm and flow. You will want to explore when and how often to engage this discipline. Some people prefer to do a daily examen, while others prefer to do it weekly.

Preparation. Spend a few moments in silence, allowing yourself to be still and know how much God loves you. Use a favorite Scripture, prayer or other spiritual reading as needed in order to settle into the assurance of God's love in the present moment. Hear God say to you, "I have loved you with an everlasting love . . ."

Invitation. Invite God to go with you in your search for evidence of his presence throughout your day and in your search for self-knowledge.

Review the day. Identify the major events of the day (or the week, if you are doing the examen weekly), including your spiritual practices, meals, appointments, interactions with others, significant events at work. Reflect on each of the events, noticing where God seemed to be loving you, speaking to you, guiding you or showing you something new about himself.

Give thanks. Thank God for each part of your day, for his presence with you in the midst of it, for those moments when you sensed a growing freedom from sin and a greater capacity to love God and others. If there are any unresolved issues or questions pertaining to the events of the day, express these to God as well, and allow yourself to experience gratitude for God's presence with you even in places that feel dark or confusing.

Confess. Using Psalm 139:23-24 as your prayer, invite God to bring to mind attitudes, actions or moments when you fell short of exhibiting the character of Christ or the fruit of the Spirit. As God brings different areas to mind, reflect on what contributed to the situation and what might enable you to respond differently in the future.

Ask forgiveness. Also express your willingness to take any concrete steps needed to allow Christ's character to be more fully formed in you. Be assured of God's forgiveness (1 John 1:9) and his power to continue leading you into the transformation you desire. Ask God if there is anything you need to do to make things right relative to the situation you have confessed.

Seek out spiritual friendship. Seek out a spiritual friend and tell them what you are discovering about yourself, your confession and your resolve to pursue transformation in this area.

> *How*
> *Did the rose*
> *Ever open its heart*
> *And give to the world*
> *All its*
> *Beauty?*
> *It felt the encouragement of light*
> *Against its*
> *Being*
> *Otherwise*
> *We all remain*
> *Too*
> *Frightened.*
>
> FROM *THE GIFT: POEMS BY HAFIZ*

7

DISCERNMENT

Recognizing and Responding to the Presence of God

*Discernment in its fullness takes a practiced heart, fine-tuned to hear
the word of God and the single-mindedness to follow that word in
love. It is truly a gift from God, but not one dropped from the skies
fully formed. It is a gift cultivated by a prayerful life and the search
for self-knowledge.*

ERNEST LARKIN

Recently I spent time with my daughter's soccer team at the beginning of a practice devoted to watching game films. We discussed the importance of game films and how it gives them the opportunity to notice mistakes they had made in the previous game (so they could do it differently next time) and also things that they had done right (so they could celebrate it and hopefully repeat it). They also noted that it gave them the opportunity to take a step back and see the field from a more complete vantage point than when they were embroiled in the heat of the game. They were able to observe the execution of plays, the overall functioning of the team, the times when they had good momentum and what contributed to the momentum, as well as those times when the energy seemed to just evaporate.

The viewing of game films is very similar to the practice of *examen* as we explored it in the previous chapter, only in this case we are viewing something so much more important than an athletic competition; we are viewing the game film of our lives! We are looking for evidence of the presence and activity of God, and we are deepening our self-awareness through self-examination. As we become more practiced, there are other very subtle dynamics we begin to notice as well that help us to discern the presence of God so that we can align ourselves more completely with God's purposes moment by moment. We begin to notice those times and moments when we were enlivened by the Spirit's life-giving energy within, and we also notice times and places where we felt drained of life in some way.

Discernment is first of all a habit, a way of seeing that eventually permeates our whole life. It is the journey from spiritual blindness (not seeing God anywhere or seeing him only where we expect to see him) to spiritual sight (finding God everywhere, especially where we least expect it). Ignatius of Loyola, founder of the Jesuits and best known for developing a set of spiritual exercises intended to hone people's capacity for this discipline, defined the aim of discernment as "finding God *in all things* in order that we might love and serve God in all" (italics mine).

The habit of discernment is a quality of attentiveness to God that is so intimate that over time we develop an intuitive sense of God's heart and purpose in any given moment. We become familiar with God's voice—the tone, quality and content—just as we become familiar with the voice of a human being we know well. We are able to grasp the answers to several key questions: Who is God for me in the moment? Where is God at work, continuing to unfold his love and redemption? Who am I most authentically in response? It is a way of looking at all of life with a view to sensing the movement of God's Spirit and abandoning ourselves to it just as we might give ourselves to the experience of floating down a river. Sometimes we lie back and allow the current of the river to carry us along. At other times it is more like trying to run the rapids or ride a large wave:

we must keep our whole self alert and attuned to the dynamic of the water as it flows over rocks, around corners and through narrow channels so that we can ride it to its destination rather than being toppled by its force. Either way, we do not set the direction or the speed of the current; rather, we seek to read the elements so that we can move with it and find the best way to let it carry us in the direction God has for us.

If we are practicing the examen of consciousness that was explored in the previous chapter, we are becoming more attuned to the presence of God, learning to notice evidence of God's presence that we might otherwise miss. Not only do these glimpses assure us of God's presence with us, they also give us hints about how he is guiding our life and an increasing sense that we really are living all of life in God.

Scripture also speaks of "discernment of spirits" and encourages us to "test the spirits to see whether they are from God" (1 Corinthians 12:10; 1 John 4:1). This aspect of discernment helps us to distinguish the real from the phony, the true from the false, in the world "out there" but also in the interior world of our thoughts and motives. It is possible for us to become so attuned to subtle spiritual dynamics that we are able to distinguish between what is good (that which moves us toward God and his calling on our life) and what is evil (that which draws us away from God).

Ignatius classifies these inner dynamics under the categories *consolation* and *desolation*. Beyond surface emotion, consolation is the interior movement of the heart that gives us a deep sense of life-giving connection with God, others and our most authentic self in God. It is the sense that in some deep way all is right with the world, that I am free to be given over to God and to love even in moments of pain and crisis. Desolation is the loss of a sense of God's presence. We feel out of touch with God, with others and with our most authentic self. In desolation we are off center, full of turmoil, confusion and maybe even rebellion. It might even be a very subtle sense of dis-ease that indicates something is amiss.

Consolation and desolation need not be particularly momentous; in fact, they might even seem relatively inconsequential until we learn to pay attention and listen for what they have to tell us. For instance, I have noticed how replenishing a particular church service is for me because of the beauty of the worship space and the depth of meaning conveyed by the religious symbols. The altar devoted to the Eucharist at the center of the worship space, the lit candles, a beautifully engraved cross, and a place to kneel at my seat or behind the altar. . . . All of this is so enlivening to me that it doesn't always matter much whether anyone says anything or not! This is a reminder that sacred space is a very significant element of worship for me and needs to be taken into account when I choose where to worship.

In the midst of a normal day of work and ministry, I will often notice that what is most enlivening to me *by far* is a quiet conversation with a friend or colleague that somehow affirms our commitment to our work and life together in community. In contrast, there might be moments in that very same day when I sensed my energy draining away due to feelings of loneliness and isolation. The deep joy that I feel in relation to my colleagues is in contrast with the desolation I feel when I am doing too much of my work in isolation, reminding me that relationships matter to me more than anything. Paying attention to these hidden inner dynamics continually guide me to be even more vigilant in choosing *for* that which life is for me. Even when the noticing is a bit painful, it speaks gently to me about my life and the importance of continuing to be more thoughtful and intentional about choosing life more consistently.

God's will for us is generally for us to pursue that which gives us life (John 10:10) and to turn away from things that drain life from us and leave us debilitated. Many of our smaller decisions and most of our significant decisions—even those that require us to choose between two equally good options—involve the ability to notice that which brings a sense of life and freedom (1 Corinthians 3:17) to our most authentic self in God. In Deuteronomy God addresses the whole company of Israel and says, "I have set before you life and death, blessings and curses. Choose life so that you and your descendants may live." He says that the wisdom that enables us to choose life is not something that we will find "out there" in heaven or across the ocean somewhere but that this knowing is very near to us—in our mouths and in our hearts for us to notice and observe (Deuteronomy 30:19-20). In other words, it is a visceral, in-the-body experience.

As we make it our habit to notice and respond to that which gives us life, receiving guidance becomes routine in the day-to-day decisions of life as well as in the larger questions of our life. It keeps us in touch with that which is truest about God, ourselves and our world so that we can make life-giving choices. Then when we are called on to make major life decisions, we can draw on this understanding and awareness to inform our choice.

This capacity to recognize and respond to the presence of God in all of life is a spiritual habit and practice that keeps us connected with God's larger purposes for us and for our world rather than being consumed by self-interest. As we become practiced at recognizing the presence and the activity of God, we are able to align ourselves more completely with what God is doing in any given moment, which is when life begins to get really exciting!

THE PRACTICE OF DISCERNMENT

Life is full of the need to choose. Sometimes the choices are momentous—choosing a marriage partner, entering a vocation, having children, what to do with a marriage that's not working. Other choices are not quite as momentous, but they are important nonetheless because they give shape to our life. Where to pursue further education, what church to attend, whether to move to a new geographical location, how to care for aging parents, appropriate sexual expression in a dating relationship, how long to stay in a marriage that's not working, whether to pursue a particular friendship or not, what spiritual practices are appropriate for my life at this time—all of these decisions shape who we are and who we are becoming.

When faced with life's choices, we become aware of another facet of the soul's deep longing: we want to know that we are making our choices in God, that we are living our life according to the purposes for which God brought us to this particular time and place. We long to see our life as part of a larger whole, contributing to some greater purpose. Within the broader Christian framework, we long to find our unique path, the one that God knew and marked out for us before the foundations of the earth. We long to experience the presence of God and respond faithfully to that presence rather than living our minutes and hours and days disconnected from spiritual reality. For lack of this kind of vision and purpose the people perish.

The need to perceive a deeper meaning for our lives is not just a midlife phenomenon. According to brain specialist Joseph Chilton Pierce, a brain spurt occurs in early adolescence related to the capacity for idealism. An adolescent's greatest developmental need is for adults whose model of a meaningful life encourages this idealism. If this capacity for idealism is not encouraged, the young person experiences profound frustration. Pierce suggests that our epidemic of teenage violence is a direct result of stunted brain growth and frustrated idealism caused by lack of meaning in the adult world that confronts them. When we move into adulthood without having discovered a deeper sense of meaning and purpose for our existence, our disillusionment can settle into a profound (and sometimes very subtle) cynicism and emotional detachment that are quite antithetical to the hope, passion and energy that are basic to our Christian faith.

FOUNDATIONS OF DISCERNMENT

While discernment is listed as a spiritual gift, it is also a mark of Christian maturity. In Romans 12:1-2 Paul is very matter-of-fact in identifying the ability to discern the will of God as a natural byproduct of spiritual transformation, and John instructs Christians in general to "test the spirits" to see which ones are from God (1 John 4:1). Whether we feel we are gifted in this area or not, discernment is a gift for all of us who are seeking the fullness of life in Christ.

For many of us, though, knowledge of God's will is a subject fraught with doubt and difficulty. Is it really possible to know the will of God? we wonder. Do I really trust him to do what's best for me? How do I know whether I have "discerned" God's will or if it is just a good way to justify what I want? How do I make sense of those times when I thought I understood the will of God but it ended up being a mess? It was hard enough to trust God the first time. How can I trust God again? As one dear friend has commented many times, "For me, finding the will of God has always been like chasing the Holy Grail. I think I'm getting closer to it, but it is always just out of reach."

In the face of such heartfelt questions, it is tempting to launch into a treatise on decision making and the will of God, but what is most needed is *a way to enter into discernment as a spiritual practice,* one that, like every other spiritual practice, offers us a way to make ourselves available for what only God can give.

The Scriptures are clear that discernment, when it is given, is always a gift. We cannot force discernment, but we can find ways to open ourselves to it. It is not accessed through a formula or a method; it is a way of being with a decision in God's presence and allowing him to guide our knowing. The capacity to discern and do the will of God arises out of friendship with God, cultivated through prayer, times of quiet listening and alert awareness.

There are at least three beliefs that are crucial for a right practice of discernment. The first is *belief in the goodness of God.* This may seem like a strange place to begin—something straight out of a first-grade Sunday school lesson—but the truth is many of us have trouble really believing in the goodness of God to us personally. We may believe in the goodness of God generally, but when it comes to the kind of belief in God's goodness that would enable me to be wide open to whatever God's will might be—well, that's a whole different story.

To really open myself to knowing and doing the will of God requires trust that God's intentions toward me are deeply good. Discernment requires *interior freedom,* a state of wide-openness to God and the capacity to relinquish whatever might keep me from choosing for God. It is the belief held deep in the core of my being that God's will is the best thing that could happen to me under any circumstances.

It is impossible to be wide open with someone you don't trust, let alone with a God whom we cannot see and whose ways we don't always understand! Subconsciously (or even consciously), we may blame God for some of the difficulties and traumas we have experienced. Though we may have a hard time admitting it, these traumas and disappointments have caused us to wonder, *Is God really good? If I trust myself to him, isn't there a good chance that I will wind up where I least want to be or that God will withhold what I want the most? Isn't God a little bit like Lucy in the Peanuts comic strip, who pulls the football away just as Charlie Brown gives himself completely to the kick, causing him to fall flat on his face?*

If we have not yet gotten to a place where we are "quite certain that there is no 'catch,' no limit, to the goodness of God's intentions or his power to carry them out," we will always hold ourselves back from being fully open to knowing the will of God.

The second foundational building block of the discernment process is the belief that *love is our primary calling.* This, too, may seem like a strange place to begin, accustomed as we are to thinking our way into decisions through intellectual exercises such as listing pros and cons. We may think our decisions are about the details of where we live, who we marry, what job we take, but for the Christian person, the choices we

make are always about love and which choice enables us to keep following God into love. There may be other factors to consider, but the deepest question for us as Christian people is, *What does love call for in this
situation? What would love do?*

Why is it that we so rarely ask this question relative to the choices we
face? What distracts us from love in various situations in which we are
trying to discern God's will? I don't know your answers to this question,
but I can tell you a few of mine. For one thing, love is a major inconvenience at times. It is rarely efficient. It is much more complicated than
just listing pros and cons and getting on with it. Furthermore, love challenges my self-centeredness, and sometimes it requires me to give more
of myself than I want to give. Sometimes love hurts, or at least it makes
me vulnerable. All the time, love is risky, and there are no guarantees.

And yet love is the deepest calling of the Christian life, the standard by
which everything about our lives is measured. It is the standard by which
Christ evaluated himself at the end of his life. "Having loved his own who
were in the world, he loved them to the end" (John 13:1). Any decision-
making process that fails to ask the love question misses the point of the
Christian practice of discernment. Discernment is intended to take us
deeper and deeper into the heart of God's will: that we would follow God
passionately into love—even if it takes us all the way to the cross.

The third foundational building block is the belief that *God does communicate with us through the Holy Spirit, and the Holy Spirit is given to help
us know the demands of love in our situation.* At the end of his life, Jesus
said that it was to our advantage that he went away, so that the Holy
Spirit could come and live with us, closer to us than our own breath.
Christ asked the Father to send the Holy Spirit to be a counselor and a
guide for us—one who leads us deeper into truth right here, right now,
as we are able to bear it. In this way the Holy Spirit expands Christ's
teaching, taking a particular teaching beyond the moment when he gave
it in a particular setting to the moment we are in right now. The Spirit is

given to help us answer the call to love in ways that are consistent with and flow out of our own personality, gifts and calling within our particular situation. We are called to live love in the context of our own destiny as freely and authentically and wholeheartedly as Christ did.

The practice of discernment assumes a deep-seated theological belief in God's presence and action through the Holy Spirit in the midst of my daily experience. It assumes that God's will is continuing to be revealed as it is needed and as I am able to hear it and respond to it.

✺ CROSSING THE THRESHOLD INTO DISCERNMENT

The practice of discernment begins with a prayer for indifference. We generally think of indifference as a negative attitude that is characterized by apathy and not caring; in the realm of discernment, however, *indifference* is a very positive term that is rich in meaning. Here it means "I am indifferent to anything but God's will." This is a state of wide-openness to God in which I am free from undue attachment to any particular outcome, and I am capable of relinquishing whatever might keep me from choosing for love. I have gotten to a place where I want God and his will more than anything—more than ego gratification, more than looking good in the eyes of others, more than personal ownership or comfort or advantage. I want "God's will, nothing more, nothing less, nothing else." For any of us human beings to come to this place of indifference is no small thing. In fact, gaining indifference is one of the most demanding aspects of the discernment process.

Mary the mother of Jesus is one of the most compelling examples of utter indifference or "given-overness" to the will of God. Despite the possibility of being ostracized by her community, judged harshly by those who didn't understand the will of God in her life, rejected by her husband-to-be, enduring inconvenience and much pain, her response to the angel who announced God's will for her life was "Here am I, the servant of the Lord; let it be with me according to your word" (Luke 1:38).

Until we have come to a place of indifference, any prayer for wisdom may well be something akin to a rigged election. Yet indifference is not easy for us to achieve—especially if we face a decision in which the outcome really matters to us or we have a vested interest in it. In fact, we are not able to achieve it at all. Just like everything else that is of significance in the spiritual life, God must accomplish this for us. That is why all we can do is pray and wait. The question that is most pertinent at this place in the discernment process is, What needs to die in me in order for God's will to come forth in my life? Is there anything I need to set aside so that I can be open to what God wants?

There are times when the answer to this question requires a kind of death, a death to self so that the life of Christ can be born more fully in us. In this spiritual death we lay down our own will in order to embrace God's will—but this is possible only if we have first possessed our own life. It is a mistake to ask people to be crucified with Christ before they have actually fully claimed their life. "The first call of the Gospel, says Teilhard de Chardin, 'is to utilize our talents, develop our gifts, and construct our human life. Only then does the call to total abnegation make sense. We are called to renounce everything and give our life totally back to God. But we must first possess that life in order to give it away.'" This was at least part of what Jesus was saying when he noted, "No one takes my life from me; I lay it down of my own accord" (John 10:18). It is not that we are devoid of our own desires; rather, we have come to a place of deep trust in the goodness of God toward us and we want his will more than anything.

Willingness to ask this question may take us into a period of waiting, in which we know we cannot accomplish for ourselves what most needs to be done. All we can say to God is "I know I am not indifferent. I know there is still something in me that is clinging to my own agenda. If I am to become indifferent, you will have to do it in me." This period of waiting may feel very dark. But strangely enough, it will also feel deeply right—as if we are right where we need to be.

The movement toward indifference is the threshold between two worlds: the world of human decision making and the world of discerning the divine will. In this waiting room of the soul we are ready to pray the second prayer—the prayer for wisdom. "If any of you is lacking in wisdom, ask God, who gives to all generously and ungrudgingly, and it will be given you" (James 1:5). Here we begin to understand why the prayer for indifference was so important: the wisdom of God is foolishness to this world. Discerning people are able to recognize God's guidance sometimes by the very fact that, to some onlookers, it appears at some level to be foolish. But because we have come to a place of indifference, it doesn't matter. When we have died to our need to be wise in others' eyes or to prove ourselves according to human standards, we are finally ready to ask for God's wisdom and receive it.

〰 Notice Without Judging

Most of us are accustomed to observing the obvious as we make decisions—circumstances, the clear meaning of pertinent Scriptures, the advice of friends who are wise in the Lord, the wisdom contained in our faith tradition. These form the basic framework for our Christian living, and it is assumed that we make decisions within this framework. Ernest Larkin, however, calls this "pre-spirituality." Discernment requires us to go beyond the basics of Christian living to notice our inner dynamics as well—dynamics such as desire and calling, consolation and desolation. These dynamics are subtle, but they give us clues as to whether the choice we are considering will nurture life in us: the life of Christ lived in and through our most authentic self.

The will of God is manifest deep within where the Spirit dwells and bears witness with our spirit about things that are true (Romans 8:16). Quaker author Thomas Kelly calls this the Light Within.

Deep within us all there is an amazing inner sanctuary of the soul, a holy place, a Divine Center, a speaking Voice to which we may continually return. Eternity is in our hearts, pressing upon our time-torn lives, warming us with intimations of an astounding destiny, calling us home unto itself. Yielding to these persuasions, gladly submitting ourselves in body and soul, utterly and completely to the Light Within is the beginning of true life.

When we have been listening to the patterns of consolation and desolation long enough, we start to come in touch with our deepest orientation and desire, some essence of ourselves that God knew before we were even created in physical form. There are desires that are deep, true and fundamental to our being in Christ; these are the "desires of your heart" that God promises to fulfill (Psalm 37:4), although often differently from how we might have envisioned. A profound life orientation is revealed in these deepest desires, and when we come in touch with them, we have found God's direction for our life. This usually also has something to do with our calling, the purpose for which God created us. This is that part of ourselves—a passion or a burden that we carry that is uniquely ours—and it cannot be set aside lightly.

Jeremiah recognized this in relation to his calling as a prophet. Midway through the book of Jeremiah, he is thoroughly disillusioned with his life as a prophet—and with good reason! He was often the bearer of bad news, he was called on to illustrate his message in ways that made him look very foolish, and he wept a lot, which is no fun for anyone! It got so bad that eventually he concluded that God had tricked him into a calling that was full of too much hardship, and he decided he wasn't going to do it anymore. But being a prophet was such an essential part of who he was that he could not set it aside.

> If I say, "I will not mention him,
>   or speak any more in his name,"
> then within me there is something like a burning fire

> shut up in my bones;
> I am weary with holding it in,
>> and I cannot. (Jeremiah 20:9)

There is something like that in all of us—something so essential to who we are and who God made us to be that we cannot set it aside without imploding. It is these kinds of inner truths that discernment requires us to pay attention to. We must have the capacity to listen to all parts of ourselves without judging them—facts that are rational and objective and feelings of consolation and desolation that are deeper than surface emotions. We must be willing to pay attention to what is conscious as well as any unconscious matter that presents itself in a dream or slips out in conversation before we have a chance to edit it. We must listen to the stirrings and the language of our desire and distinguish our desires from the wants and shoulds of our lives. "Wants are mine; shoulds are somebody else's."

GATHER AND ASSESS THE DATA

In the realm of spiritual transformation, the questions we are willing to ask ourselves are more important than the answers we think we know. At no time is this truer than when we are involved in discernment. There are many questions that can help us to reflect on the objective facts and gain insight into any deeper dynamics involved in a decision as we reflect on them in God's presence. It is important to resist the tendency to approach such questions in a purely linear, academic fashion, as though trying to complete an assignment; rather we enter into these questions as a spiritual practice, asking God to draw us to those that will be most helpful in bringing clarity to our situation. At different times, different questions will resonate and help us to attend to the ways in which God's will is manifest deep in our being.

Direction and calling. How does this choice fit with the overall direction and calling of God on my life? (Remember Jeremiah's experience of calling.) Is there one word that captures my sense of calling these days? Does the current choice enable me to continue living into my calling?

Consolation and desolation. Which choice brings the deepest sense of life, inner peace and freedom (John 10:10; 2 Corinthians 3:17)? Is there a growing sense of wholeness, authenticity, congruence with who I am in God? Or might this decision draw me away from God?

Scripture. Is there a particular Scripture that God is bringing to me relative to this choice? What is it saying to me?

Life of Christ. Is this choice consistent with what I know of the mind and heart of Christ and his redemptive purposes in the world?

Character growth and development. How will this direction nurture the fruit of the Spirit in me—particularly the fruit of love? What does love call for? What is God doing in my character and spiritual growth? Will this choice continue to nurture this growth?

Eternal perspective. Does this choice reflect the value of what is eternal and permanent and holds the deepest value rather than what is transient and impermanent? On my deathbed, which choice would I wish I had made?

Community. How does this choice fit with others' observations of who I am and what God is doing in my life? Am I willing to open up every facet of this decision to a trusted spiritual friend for their wisdom and insight? Is there anything in the broad tradition of the Christian faith that might inform my decision?

When we come to a point at which discernment is especially needed, we may need to seek extra solitude so that we have the time and space for silent listening around these and similar questions. Jesus himself was very intentional about setting aside times of solitude for intense prayer and listening to God at important choice points in his life. The very beginnings of his public ministry came as a result of his listening to the voice of his Father affirm his identity as a beloved son. In Matthew 4 we find him in the wilderness struggling with subtle temptations regarding his calling. Would he carry out his calling according to what he understood from God, or would he follow a path that made more sense from a human standpoint? In Luke 6 we observe Jesus' choice to spend the night alone in prayer before choosing his key disciples—certainly one of the most important decisions of his life in ministry. Luke 22 recounts another night spent in solitude, when Jesus struggled mightily with his choice to go to the cross. In the Garden of Gethsemane he poured out his heart to God, and he did not stop until he had wrestled all the way through it, becoming certain that this was God's will and he was ready to submit himself to it. If Jesus felt the need for presence to God in solitude as a context for discernment, it is certain that we need it as well.

Seek Inner Confirmation

At some point, a way ahead starts to become clear. There may even be a couple of options that seem equally good. Now God invites us to make a choice—at least interiorly—and to seek inner confirmation. Again we rely on the dynamics of consolation and desolation. We make a choice inside of ourselves first and take some time to live with our choice privately and see whether there is a sense of rightness about it, a sense of being in harmony with myself—the person God created me to be and the person I want to be. We can take several days to live as if we had made a certain decision and notice whether there is a sense of life and sustaining energy.

During this time we can ask ourselves what is the truest and most authentic expression of the Spirit in and through my life *at this time.* It is important to recognize in what part of myself this peace and consolation rests. Is the ego part of me at peace because I am choosing something that will keep the ego in control? Is it the fearful part of me that is at peace, because I am choosing a path that keeps me safe and secure? Or does this peace reside in the deepest, truest part of me—the part that has the capacity and willingness to be completely given over to God? If we are trying to decide between two options, we can then take several days to walk around as if we had made the other choice and notice the same dynamic.

When we attend to these different dimensions of ourselves, we begin to understand that this way of discerning

> depends greatly on our spiritual and psychological maturity. If we are ambivalent and divided by chaotic emotions and neurotic conditions, our affective states will provide no positive guidance. Our task will be to understand our condition and bring order and discipline into our affective life. But as we come to achieve that discipline, in proportion as "we die and our lives are lives hidden with Christ in God," [discernment] becomes more effective.

Just Do It!

Once we have asked God for wisdom and we are at least clear on the next step in following God's will for our life (God rarely gives us more than the next step!), there is nothing left but to follow God's will to the best of our ability. This will involve making plans and working hard to implement those plans, but now all of our planning is done with a sense that God is in it, leading us along, and that we are connected with his larger purposes for our life.

Discernment is risky, and there are no guarantees; we can never be absolutely sure that we have discerned everything correctly. We are, after all, limited and fallen. But what we can know for sure is that God is with us, that the desire to please God does, in fact, please him, and that he will never leave us or forsake us. That is the most important thing we need to know.

Discernment as a Way of Life in God

Ultimately, discernment is about falling in love and letting that decide everything. It is about falling so deeply in love with God that nothing else matters. It is about trusting God so much that all we want in this life is to abandon ourselves to the goodness of his will. It is about knowing God so intimately that we can tell what he wants just by turning our heart toward him. It is about loving ourselves and God and others so much that we will wait until we understand what love calls us to and then give ourselves to it, even when it costs us.

> Nothing is more practical than finding God, than falling in love in a quite absolute, final way. What you are in love with, what seizes your imagination, will affect everything else. It will decide what will get you out of bed in the morning, what you will do with your evening, how you spend your weekend, what you read, whom you know, what breaks your heart, and what amazes you with joy and gratitude. Fall in love, stay in love, and it will decide everything.

❧ Practice

Part 1: The Habit of Discernment

As a way of cultivating the habit of discernment, take a few moments in your solitude times to notice the dynamics of consolation and desolation. This kind of noticing can easily be incorporated into the practice of examen that was explored in the previous chapter. The following exercise is adapted from *Sleeping with Bread* by Dennis Linn, Sheila Fabricant Linn and Matthew Linn.

Ask God to bring to your heart a moment in the last few days for which you are most grateful. When were you most able to give and receive love? Which moment seemed to have the most life in it for you? What was said or done that made it life giving for you?

Ask God to bring to your heart a moment in the last few days for which you are *least* grateful. When were you least able to give and receive love? Which moment seemed to drain life from you? What was said or done that made it so draining for you?

What wisdom, insight or further questions seem to arise from this awareness? How might God be inviting you to incorporate into your life more of that which gives you life and less of that which drains life from you?

Thank God for his presence with you during this time and for whatever wisdom, guidance and questions that came.

Part 2: The Practice of Discernment

Are you facing a decision right now that warrants entering into a process of discernment? If so, identify the question or choice point for which you are seeking God's wisdom, and move through the process described in this chapter. This may take weeks, days or even months depending on the magnitude of the decision you are facing.

Remember, although the prayer for indifference and the prayer for wisdom initiate the discernment process, the order of the rest of the elements is not necessarily linear. You may experience them more in a creative mix, working together in different ways, as you continue to bring this decision into God's presence and pay attention to the insight that comes. You may need to expand your periods of solitude in order to have time and space for working through the different elements described in this chapter.

Identify the issue or question for discernment, and notice whether you are confident of God's good intentions toward you in this area and whether you feel you can trust him. Notice how deeply you are committed to love at this time and whether you have confidence in the Holy Spirit's presence to guide you. Take time to be with God with what is true about you relative to these foundational building blocks of discernment.

Notice whether or not you are indifferent to anything but the will of God. If not, tell God about your concerns, your inability to let go, your attachment to particular outcomes, and ask him to help you to become indifferent. Wait on God for this; when you have been able to loosen your grip on the outcomes, pray and ask God for wisdom (James 1:5).

Take time (days or weeks, whatever it takes) to notice without judging and journal about all that you are noticing. Assess the meaning of what you are noticing as you go along, and reflect on the questions in this chapter that draw you. When you feel you've gathered enough information, you may want to synthesize it, talk about what you are noticing with a spiritual friend and invite their feedback.

As one or two paths become clear, seek inner confirmation by taking several days to "walk around as if" you had made a particular decision and notice whether there is a sense of inner peace and freedom.

When you have come to a sense of peace about a particular choice or direction, enter into it knowing that God is with you and that he will complete the work he has begun in you.

"My Lord God, I have no idea where I am going. I do not see the road ahead of me. I cannot know for certain where it will end. Nor do I really know myself. And the fact that I think I am following your will does not mean I am actually doing so. But I believe that the desire to please you does in fact please you. And I hope I have that desire in everything I am doing. I hope that I will never do anything apart from that desire and I know that if I do this you will lead me by the right road, though I may know nothing about it. Therefore I will trust you always though I may seem to be lost and in the shadow of death. I will not fear, for you are ever with me, and you will never leave me to face my perils alone."

THOMAS MERTON, *THOUGHTS IN SOLITUDE*

8

SABBATH

Establishing Rhythms of Work and Rest

If you refrain from trampling the sabbath,
   from pursuing your own interests on my holy day;
if you call the sabbath a delight
   and the holy day of the LORD honorable;
if you honor it, not going your own ways,
   serving your own interests, or pursuing your own affairs;
then you shall take delight in the LORD,
   and I will make you ride upon the heights.

ISAIAH 58:13-14

Several years ago I was run over by a car while riding my bike. Actually, it was a minivan driven by an elderly man whose reflexes were not what they used to be. He was stopped, waiting to pull out of a parking lot, and I was riding on the sidewalk that passed in front of it. Instead of remaining stopped and yielding the right of way, he began pulling out of the driveway just as I was crossing in front of him.

It was one of those slow-motion moments: I could see what was about to happen but couldn't do anything to stop it. We collided, I fell, and his front tires drove onto my legs (which were still intertwined with the bike) and actually came to rest on top of my legs. He threw the car into reverse and the back tires spun because they couldn't get traction. There was this moment of utter stillness and clarity when I thought, *I hope he gets his car off me soon, because this really hurts.*

To make a long story short, he was able to back the car off me, but he was so dazed by what had happened that he got out and wandered into the street, not knowing what to do. Fortunately, an ambulance "just happened" to be passing by, and the paramedics jumped out, scooped me up off the pavement, put me in the ambulance and whisked me away to the emergency room. In what could have been a devastating accident, I ended up with only cuts and bruises and a fractured ankle.

The first feeling to set in as I got situated back at home was euphoria. If there had been a moment's difference in the timing, my whole body could have been run over rather than just my legs, so I was grateful to be alive and in one piece. The doctors expressed amazement that my legs had been able to hold up under the weight of the vehicle. Needless to say, our family sat around that night wide-eyed with relief, realizing that the outcome could have been altogether different.

But eventually the relief gave way to other levels of awareness. One friend, after expressing his initial concern, laughingly commented, "Ruth, when are you going to learn that when you're on a bike, you can't take on a van?" Another friend, concerned that I wasn't taking time to fully recover, said, "You know, you really are allowed to take a break; you did just get run over by a car!" And then there was this sentence from Wayne Muller's book *Sabbath* that kept buzzing around in my head like a pesky fly buzzing against a windowpane: "If we do not allow for a rhythm of rest in our overly busy lives, illness becomes our Sabbath— our pneumonia, our cancer, our heart attack, our accidents create Sabbath for us."

I did not want to hear this. I did not want to consider the fact that perhaps this accident, while it was not God's fault, was a way God was trying to tell me something. I did not want to acknowledge the possibility that it was that hard for God to get my attention. I did not want to

face the fact that for years I had been thumbing my nose at human limitations, behaving as though I was beyond needing a sabbath. (It was a
nice thought for retired people or people who weren't all that busy, but
I wasn't one who *needed* a sabbath.)

The other part of the truth is that, up to that point, I really hadn't been
willing to enter all the way into the longing and impossibility that the
idea of sabbath stirred up in me. Sabbath was something I knew about
and had read about—and, honestly, it was some of the most stirring
writing I had ever read. Writings about the sabbath were the only writings that made me weep—with longing and also with sadness that I had
no idea how to make it happen meaningfully in my own life. Muller's de-
scriptions of sabbath practices had been so moving that I could read his
book only a little at a time.

> Light a candle, alone or with friends. Let each of you speak about
> those things that are left to do, and as the candle burns, allow the
> cares to melt away. Do no be anxious about tomorrow, said Jesus.
> The worries of today are sufficient for today. Whatever remains to
> be done, for now, let it be. It will not get done tonight. In Sabbath
> time we take our hand off the plow, and allow God and the earth
> to care for what is needed. Let it be . . .

Gentle instructions like these were almost more than I could bear. Nothing in my life was that gentle.

Something about the beauty and the kindness and the concreteness
of it all pierced my self-sufficiency and melted the hardness of my activism; all I wanted to do was fall down and worship a God who would
think to give us such a gift. All I could do was weep at the beauty of these
truths and symbolic actions, weep because so few of us—and least of all
I—are courageous enough to live in this beautiful way. What an amazing
thing it would be to have the rhythms of your life regularly usher you
into such deep trust that you could actually rest from it all. Who would

we be, who would I be, if I trusted like this for twenty-four hours once a week?

I also didn't want to wrestle with the issues that I knew sabbath would raise in my life. At that point, Sunday was anything but a day of rest in our family. Let's face it: for church people it is a day for highly programmed services, youth programs, committee meetings, membership classes and small groups that wear everyone out and keep family members coming and going all day. For consumers, Sunday is a day to shop. For working people, it is a time to catch up and do all the errands and household chores that are missed during the week. For athletes and their families, it is a day for packing chairs, bags and water bottles and traveling far and wide to sporting events. I just did not know how to try to incorporate this radical discipline into my life in the midst of a culture that knows nothing of setting aside a whole day to rest and delight in God. What a messy can of worms this was going to open up!

Listening to Our Longings

The truth is, sabbath keeping is a discipline that will mess with you, because once you move beyond just thinking about it and actually begin to practice it, the goodness of it will capture you, body, soul and spirit. You will long to wake up to a day that stretches out in front of you with nothing in it but rest and delight. You will long for a simple way to turn your heart toward God in worship without much effort. You will long for a space in time when the pace is slow and family and friends linger with one another, savoring one another's presence because no one has anywhere else to go.

You will long to sit on your own couch or on your own deck because it is yours, a gift from God that often gets overlooked in the rush of things. You will long for the day when you can crawl back into bed for an afternoon nap, which is all the more delicious because on this day you know that you are doing exactly what God wants you to do. (This is the one time when "oughts" and "shoulds" are just wonderful!) You will long for that leisurely walk or bike ride. You will long for the experience of preparing your favorite foods and sharing them with people you love. You will long to read a book for pleasure.

You will long to light candles and read Scripture and thank God from the bottom of your heart. You will long to feel the quietness and peace settle over your house as you and your family enter into a different way of being together in God's presence. You will long for a few others who understand the beauty of sabbath time and will practice it with you. You will long for a community whose traditions enable you to honor the sabbath rather than making it a day of Christian busyness. You will long for a rhythm of working and resting that you can count on.

During the week, your whole self will strain toward the sabbath with thoughts like *I know I can make it because the sabbath is coming.* You will emerge from sabbath with renewed energy and hope, thinking, *I can face my life now because I have rested.* The sabbath will become the centerpiece of your week, the kingpin of your spiritual rhythms. And when even an hour of it is robbed from you, you will grieve its loss. When you miss it, it will hurt.

Or at least that is what has happened to me.

⚛ SABBATH: A SANCTUARY IN TIME

Sabbath keeping is more than just taking a day of rest; it is a way of ordering one's life around a pattern of working six days and then resting on the seventh. It is a way of arranging our life to honor the rhythm of things—work and rest, fruitfulness and dormancy, giving and receiving, being and doing, activism and surrender. The day itself is set apart, devoted completely to rest, worship and delighting in God, but the rest of the week must be lived in such a way as to make sabbath possible. Paid work needs to be contained to five days of the week. Household chores, shopping and errand-running need to be complete before the sabbath comes, or they must wait. Courageous decisions need to be made about work and athletics, church and community involvement.

As we consider making such changes, it is important to realize that this pattern of giving one-seventh of our time back to God is woven deep into the fabric of Christian tradition and is found in some form in most of the world's spiritual traditions. It is a pattern that God himself established as he was doing the work of creation, and it was incorporated into Jewish tradition in such a way as to order the Jews' whole existence as a nation.

For Jewish folks, sabbath observance began on Friday evening and ended on Saturday evening, providing a sanctuary in time even during seasons in their history when they had no physical sanctuary. The practice of keeping the sabbath holy and completely set apart was and still is at the heart of their national identity. Far beyond mere duty and obligation, they even have special words and metaphors to express an emotion that is almost too deep to be expressed: the love of the sabbath. This was the same emotion found in medieval literature's references to the chivalrous love that knights felt for their ladies.

Of course, we have all heard about or even experienced the extreme of joyless sabbaths filled with dour prohibitions and somber rituals. But this is only a human distortion. The ancient rabbis knew that while sabbath demanded "all of man's attention, the service and devotion of total love . . . the Sabbath is the most precious present mankind has received from the treasure house of God." Of the place of sabbath in Jewish tradition, Abraham Heschel writes, "It was as if a whole people were in love with the seventh day."

I know this emotion, for I have felt it.

In the Christian church we have shifted our day of worship to Sunday in order to commemorate Jesus' resurrection weekly; it's a great idea, but something has certainly gotten lost in the translation. Most Christians don't even think about the resurrection on a normal Sunday, and we certainly have not created any sort of sanctuary in time that provides us with a whole day to rest and delight in God.

Lauren Winner, a converted Jew, captures the difference between the Christian Sunday and the Jewish sabbath as she experienced it one Sunday afternoon after church. On a visit to her favorite coffee house, she stumbled across a book about one woman's conversion to Judaism. Here is how the book's author described her experience with sabbath: "Shabbat is like nothing else. Time as we know it does not exist for these twenty-four hours, and the worries of the week soon fall away. A feeling of joy appears. The smallest object, a leaf or a spoon, shimmers in a soft light, and the heart opens. Shabbat is a meditation of unbelievable beauty."

Winner contrasts that with her own experience of sitting in the Mud-house coffee shop on this Sunday afternoon. "It was not an ordinary work-day and I did feel somewhat more relaxed than on Monday morning," she notes. "But it was not Shabbat. Nan Fink nailed it: Shabbat is like nothing else. And Shabbat is, without question, the piece of Judaism I miss the most. . . . The Sabbath is a basic unit of Christian time, a day the Church, too, tries to devote to reverence of God and rest from toil. And yet here a Sunday afternoon finds me sitting in a coffee shop, spending money, scribbling in the margins of my book, very much in 'time as we know it,' not at all sure that I have opened my heart in any particular way."

I know that feeling too, for I have felt it.

Just this past Sunday we tried desperately to carve out sabbath time in our family's hectic life and could come up with only two hours when we could all be together and life could feel any different from the way it usually does. Church activities, one daughter's meeting for a ministry she was beginning, another daughter's basketball game (a tournament final, of course), another daughter's travel plans, a work commitment for my husband and my own book deadline combined to make sabbathing impossible. What we ended up with was two hours to have dinner together, and even that was made possible only because several of us shifted our schedules and canceled things. It was delightful to be together, but it did not have that set-apart quality of the sabbath when time itself changes, when we settle into a kinder, gentler way of being and our hearts soften and open.

There *is* a difference. For I have also experienced the utter joy and relief when sabbath does happen, when the house has been cleaned, special food has been bought, the computer has been turned off, the last obligation has been completed or set aside, the candles or the fireplace has been lit, and it is time to stop, whether everything has been finished or not. I know what it is like to rest for hours until I have energy to delight in something—good food, a good book, a leisurely walk, a long-awaited conversation with someone I love. I know what it's like to feel joy and hope and peace flow back into my body and soul though I had thought it might never come again. I know what it's like to see my home and my children through the sabbath eyes of enjoyment. I know what it's like to have rest turn into delight, and delight turn into gratitude, and gratitude into worship. I know what it is like to recover myself so completely that I am able, by God's grace, to enter into my work on Monday with a renewed sense of God's calling and God's presence.

How could you not love a day that does all that? How could you not sell everything you have for this pearl of great price?

Honoring the Limits of Our Humanness

The point of the sabbath is to honor our need for a sane rhythm of work and rest. It is to honor the body's need for rest, the spirit's need for replenishment and the soul's need to delight itself in God for God's own sake. It begins with a willingness to acknowledge the limits of our humanness and take steps to live more graciously within the order of things.

And the first order of things is that we are creatures and God is the Creator. God is the only One who is infinite. I am finite, which means that I live within physical limits of time and space and bodily limits of strength and energy. There are limits to my capacities relationally, emotionally, mentally and spiritually. I am not God. God is the One who can be all things to all people. God is the One who can be two places at once. God is the One who never sleeps. I am not.

This is pretty basic stuff, but many of us live as though we don't know it. If we dig down a little deeper, we may see that our unwillingness to practice sabbath is really an unwillingness to live within the limits of our humanity, to honor our finiteness. We cling to some sense that we are indispensable and that the world cannot go on without us even for a day. Or we feel that certain tasks and activities are more significant than the delights that God is wanting to share with us. This is a grandiosity that we indulge to our own peril.

There is something deeply spiritual about honoring the limitations of our existence as human beings—physical bodies in a world of time and space. A peace descends upon our lives when we accept what is real rather than always pushing beyond our limits. Something about being gracious and accepting and gentle with ourselves at least once a week enables us to be more gracious and accepting and gentle with others. There is a freedom that comes from being who we are in God and resting in God that eventually enables us to bring something truer to the world than all of our doing. Sabbath keeping helps us to live within our limits, because on the sabbath, in many different ways, we allow ourselves to be the creature in the presence of our Creator. We touch something more real in ourselves and others than what any of us is able to produce. We touch our very being in God.

∾ GETTING STARTED

I think Jewish folks had it right: the only way to even begin the first halting steps toward a true sabbath practice is to let yourself fall in love with this day so that you long for it as you would a lover. But to fall in love with it you have to try it.

But this raises many questions for us, both theological and practical.

Does it matter what day of the week we practice sabbath? Can I have a floating sabbath, fitting it in wherever I can in a given week? Did Jesus teach sabbath keeping as a practice for New Testament Christians? Does sabbath have to be a full day, or can it just be an afternoon or an evening? Can I shop or mow the lawn on the sabbath? How do I know what I should and should not do on the sabbath?

All of these are valid questions. Some of them lie beyond the scope of this book, but let me offer several principles that, for me, undergird the whole sabbath experience. First, the heart of sabbath is that we cease our work so that we can rest and delight in God and God's good gifts. Everything we might choose to do or not to do needs to somehow fit into these purposes. Second, it is important to establish a regular rhythm if at all possible. The human being, body and soul, responds to rhythms and is accustomed to living in rhythms—night and day, three meals a day, the seasons of the year. Part of the restfulness of sabbath is knowing that it is always coming in the same interval, so that we're not making decisions about it every week. When sabbath is not observed on the same day every week, it means that we go longer than seven days without a sabbath, and that is not optimal. After seven days without rest, we are at risk of becoming dangerously tired.

> Because we do not rest, we lose our way. We miss the compass points that would show us where to go, we bypass the nourishment that would give us succor. We miss the quiet that would give us wisdom. We miss the joy and love born of effortless delight. Poisoned by this hypnotic belief that good things come only through unceasing determination and tireless effort, we can never truly rest. And for want of rest our lives are in danger.

The third principle that has become foundational for me as I have lived this discipline is that sabbath keeping is not primarily a private, self-indulgent discipline. It is and always has been a communal discipline, or at least a discipline that people enter into with those closest to them.

I am concerned when people take their sabbath on a day when their family is not able to engage it with them. I know why they do it, and I have been tempted to do it myself. Family life is sometimes part of what wearies us, and we fear that the effort required to harness a whole family to practice sabbath would take more from us than it could possibly replenish. However, if we are Christian parents or live in any kind of a family unit, we have to consider the ramifications of making sabbath simply a private discipline. Our children will then not have the opportunity to experience sabbath time with the guidance of their parents, they will not learn how to rest and delight in God (and they so desperately need it), and the special gifts of sabbath time—the quality of presence to each other, the love that is shared, the gratitude toward God, the opportunity to rest and do all those things that are counter to life in our culture—are lost to the next generation.

The other thing that's lost to the next generation is experiencing the quality of our presence on the sabbath. I am different on the sabbath. We all are. We move more slowly. We are more available to each other in terms of our time and also in terms of our attention and spirit. We are much more in touch with the softer, more vulnerable part of ourselves, because we're not pushing so hard.

Since we started our sabbath practice somewhat late in our family's life, it has been quite an adjustment. But once our daughters began to get used to it, I have seen them really enjoy the differences that are present on this day. They seem to love the fact that I'm home all day and that we can talk and take walks and cook their favorite foods. They love the fact that we all take naps and that we can go with the flow. Now they, too, articulate their need for a day to rest and are disappointed when something in their own lives or ours robs us of this important time.

🐝 Shaping Sabbath Time: What to Exclude

We can begin shaping our sabbath by deciding what should be excluded from this day and what should be included. There are at least three categories of things that we do well to exclude from our sabbath.

Work. What constitutes work for us? We must commit ourselves to not doing these things on the sabbath. We need to identify the challenges and temptations related to our work and establish clear boundaries to protect sabbath time. The greatest challenge for me is having a home office, which means that my work is facing me all the time. It is a great temptation to check e-mail and voicemail (just once) or to try to get writing and speaking prep done (just a little), yet computers and most communication technologies take me back into work mode and are deadening to my spirit. They serve good purposes during the work week, but in the context of sabbath they are a real intrusion and do not usher me into trust and rest. To interrupt my work patterns in order to take a sabbath, I have had to close the door and not even go into my office on the sabbath. Over time, though, the attraction to work on the sabbath has lessened greatly, so I don't have to be as rigid about avoiding that room.

We also need to pay attention to whether a particular activity triggers our activism, our need to be productive in order to feel worthwhile, or our feelings of indispensability. Yard work may be restful for some, but for others it is one more thing to check off the to-do list, and that is not what sabbath is about. Real discernment is needed to recognize these inner dynamics and make sabbath decisions accordingly.

Buying and selling. If we are out buying, selling and engaging in the world of commerce, it means someone has to work and we are contributing to it. It also feeds our consumerism—an aspect of life in our culture that needs rest on the sabbath. The world of commerce functions on the basis of enticing us to think we need things we don't really need and convincing us to buy things we can't really afford. It is a world designed to keep us overstimulated so that we are never satisfied and are unable to delight in the gifts of God that money cannot buy. To abstain from being a consumer on this day sensitizes us to the more substantive gifts of God in our lives.

Worry. There are more kinds of work than just physical work. There is also the emotional and mental hard work that we are engaged in all week long as we try to figure out everything in our life and make it all work. The sabbath is an invitation to rest emotionally and mentally from things that cause worry and stress. Taxes, budgets, to-do lists, wedding planning, major decision making and the like should be saved for another time. If we observe sabbath on Sunday, perhaps Sunday evening after dinner is a time when, from a place of rest, we can engage in some of the decision making that needs to be done.

✸ SHAPING SABBATH TIME: WHAT TO INCLUDE

What is to replace all that we are excluding from our sabbath time? The simple answer is *whatever delights you and replenishes you.*

Resting the body. What are the activities that rest and replenish your body? The invitation of sabbath time is to replace the time you would normally spend working with activities that you find restorative: a nap, a walk, a bike ride, a long bubble bath, eating your favorite foods (no dieting on the sabbath), sitting in the sun, lighting candles, listening to beautiful music, lovemaking. In Jewish tradition, Winner points out, married couples get rabbinical brownie points for having sex on the sabbath. You've gotta love a religion like that!

Replenishing the spirit. Another invitation of the sabbath is to pay attention to what replenishes the spirit and choose only those activities that renew you and bring you joy. Obviously, this is highly personal to each one of us; it is amazing to have permission to pay attention to what delights you and choose that on this day. As you explore this aspect of sabbath, pay close attention to those activities that merely stimulate you or serve as fillers and those things that really replenish you. Usually television and most things technological are not really replenishing; they are merely distractions from God's more meaningful gifts.

My favorite thing to do on the sabbath is quite simple. In my office I have a really comfortable couch right in front of a sunny window facing a garden. I love to lie on the couch under a quilt (not a blanket but a quilt, because I love quilts) and read a book for pleasure. On a really good sabbath I will get to do this for several hours. The couch is so comfortable and restful for my body. I have many symbols and religious artifacts in my office that delight me and speak to me about God. And since I love words but spend much time *working* with words, reading for the sheer pleasure of it is the most delicious thing I could choose. I also love it when members of my family come into that space and sit and talk with me quietly. This rarely happens in the six-day rush of things, and it replenishes me deep inside.

Restoring the soul. Perhaps the deepest refreshment is the invitation to renew the soul through worship and quiet reflection. This is the part of us that gets most lost during the work week, which is governed almost completely by the value of productivity. Of course, you will want to include worship in community, but it is also good to incorporate some aspect of worship that is more personal to you and to your family into your sabbath observance. On your own you may be able to spend some extra time in silence and prayer, take a slow, meditative walk, read a book that God has been using in your life, journal about your week, or do an extended version of the examen of consciousness with particular attention to those things you are grateful for. As a family (if your children are old enough), maintain a quieter and more spacious feeling in your home on the sabbath. Pay attention to how you can express love to each other on this day. Identify rituals or shared activities that create a spirit of reverence for God on this day—have a special meal preceded by a Scripture reading; light candles and go around the table and talk about where God seemed particularly present with you during the week; turn off the TV and talk with each other; take a walk together after dinner; play games; write or call far-away loved ones; open your home to friends, family or neighbors.

Do not make sabbath keeping a weighty exercise. Explore it with delight, as though you and God are learning together how to make the day special for both of you. Then, be as intentional about protecting it as you can be, but do not become rigid and legalistic about it, which ruins the spirit of the day. "The sabbath was made for human beings, not human beings for the sabbath" (Mark 2:27).

A FULLNESS IN TIME

I do not know everything there is to know about sabbath; in this discipline as much as any other, I am a beginner. What I do know is there have to be times in your life when you move slow . . . times when you walk rather than run, allowing your body to settle into each step . . . times when you sit and gaze admiringly at loved ones, rather than racing through an agenda . . . times when you receive food and drink with gratitude and humility rather than gulping it down on your way to something "more important." Times when hugs linger and kisses are real.

There have to be times when you read for the sheer pleasure of it, marveling at the beauty of words and writers' endless creativity in putting them together. There have to be times when you sink into the comforts of home and become human again rather than using home as a hotel or a fast-food restaurant; times when you light a candle and find the place inside you that loves and then pray out of that place. There have to be times when you let yourself feel what you feel, when you let tears come rather than blinking them back because you don't have time to cry. There have to be times to be the creature—softer, more vulnerable and more human—rather than always being tough, defended and in control.

There have to be times to sit with your gratitude for the good gifts in your life that get forgotten in the rush.

To celebrate
  and play
    and roll down hills
      and splash in water
        and spread paint on paper or walls or each other.

There have to be times to sit and wait for the fullness of God that replenishes body, mind and soul—if you can even stand to be so full. There has to be time for the fullness of time, or time is meaningless.

❧ PRACTICE

As you finish reading this chapter, take a few moments to listen to your longings regarding the sabbath. Where did you feel a keen desire for the rhythms and practices described here? Where did you feel resistance? Or if you didn't feel anything, notice that too. For several days at least, use your time in quiet to just sit with your own longings and the issues they raise for you.

Then, based on your desire and situation, decide to try one sabbath. You don't have to change your whole life—yet. Just look on your calendar for one day of the week that is realistic for you and your family to set aside for sabbath. Consider what preparations and planning are necessary for making sure that you set aside all types of work and worry on this day.

- What activities will I refuse to engage in so that it is truly a day of rest, worship and delight?

- What activities bring me delight, and how will I incorporate them? (Do not plan it out too precisely; gather some ideas—like when you will go to church or who you will include in your day—but give yourself one day to feel what it's like to wake up and know that this is a day for you to rest and follow your bliss.)

- Put the date on your calendar, and pray that God will help you to honor this sabbath and keep it holy.

Then just see where it starts to lead you.

9

A RULE OF LIFE

Cultivating Rhythms for
Spiritual Transformation

We long to see our lives whole, to know that they matter. We wonder whether our many activities might ever come together in a way of life that is good for ourselves and others. Lacking a vision of a life-giving way of life, we turn from one task to another, doing as well as we can but increasingly uncertain about what doing things well would look like. We yearn for a deeper understanding of how to order human life in accord with what is true and good.

CRAIG DYKSTRA AND DOROTHY BASS,
PRACTICING OUR FAITH

Living into what we want in any area of our life requires some sort of intentional approach. Building a solid financial base, retirement planning, home improvements, career advancement, further education, losing weight or becoming more fit—all of these require a plan if we are to make any progress in achieving what we desire. The desire for a way of life that creates space for God's transforming work is no different. However, if we look closely at the way we live day to day, we may well notice that our approach to spiritual transformation is much more random and haphazard than our approach to finances, home improvements and weight loss! Many of us try to shove spiritual transformation into the nooks and crannies of a life that is already unmanageable, rather than being willing to arrange our life for what our heart most wants. We think that somehow we will fall into transformation by accident.

Jesus had something to say about this. He used parables to picture a person who has searched long and hard for something very valuable and very special. In one story the prized item is a piece of land; in another it is a valuable pearl. In both stories, the merchant has been looking for this prize all his life, and when he finds it, he doesn't hesitate. He sells everything he has so that he can buy what he has been searching for.

Both the field and the pearl are metaphors for the kingdom of God—that state of being in which God is reigning in our life and his presence is shaping our reality. The kingdom of God is here now, if we are willing to arrange our life to embrace it. Paul speaks in passionate terms of using every ounce of his energy and intentionality to present every person mature in Christ—beginning, presumably, with himself. The only question, it seems, is, How bad do you want it?

Christian tradition has a name for the structure that enables us to say yes to the process of spiritual transformation day in and day out. It is called *a rule of life*. A rule of life seeks to respond to two questions: Who do I want to be? How do I want to live? Actually, it might be more accurate to say that a rule of life seeks to address the interplay between these two questions: *How do I want to live so I can be who I want to be?*

St. Benedict was the first one to develop a rule of life, to help monks who were living in community to order their days very simply around three key elements of their life in God: prayer, study and work. St. Benedict's Rule, like any rule of life, is simply a pattern of attitudes, behaviors and practices that are regular and routine and are intended to produce a certain quality of life and character. I prefer the language of rhythm because it speaks of regularity that the body and soul can count on, but it also speaks of ebb and flow, creativity and beauty, music and dancing, joy and giving ourselves over to a force or a power that is beyond ourselves and is deeply good. Over time, as we surrender ourselves to new life rhythms, they help us to surrender old behaviors, attitudes and practices so that we can be shaped by new ones.

❧ DEVELOPING A RHYTHM OF SPIRITUAL PRACTICES

Developing a rhythm of spiritual practices takes time. It takes time to explore a variety of disciplines so that you have some sense of their meaning for your life and how you might incorporate them realistically. It takes time to learn how to arrange them in a way that fits your life and also has beauty, like a dance or a beautifully arranged symphony or the ebb and flow of seasons and tides. It's best to try each discipline one at a time and work with it for a while rather than trying to load on too much all at once. Once you have experienced the basic disciplines, as we have done in previous chapters, you are in a position to arrange your life around the practices that open you to intimacy with God that results in the kind of change your heart is longing for.

An effective rhythm of spiritual practices will be very *personal*. No two individuals will have exactly the same rhythm, because no two people are alike. Your rhythm of spiritual practices will take into account your personality, your spiritual type, your season of life, the sin patterns you are contending with, the places where you know God is trying to stretch you. For instance, a relatively unstructured, spontaneous personality will need to be careful not to craft a rhythm of life that feels too structured and confining. A person who is more structured and enjoys closure will probably like having things mapped out in more detail.

We can also choose disciplines that address the areas of sin and negative patterns that God is helping us to become aware of. If we are becoming aware that we lack discipline in our speaking and interacting with others—prone to gossip or empty chatter, cynicism or meanness—then God might be inviting us into the discipline of silence. If we are aware of a driven quality in our life and work, the daily discipline of solitude plus the weekly discipline of sabbath may be an emphasis for us. If we notice that we are having problems in one or several of our relationships, an emphasis on self-examination may be needed. All of the disciplines described in this book are basic Christian disciplines that we all need; however, at different times different ones need to be emphasized based on the need of the moment.

Our rhythm of spiritual practices also needs to be ruthlessly *realistic* in view of our stage of life. A married couple with young children will have radically different rhythms from those of the retired couple whose children have left the nest. If we do not take into account a realistic assessment of our stage of life, we are doomed to fail.

One of the great temptations of the spiritual life is to believe that if I were in another season of life, I could be more spiritual. The truth is that spiritual transformation takes place as we embrace the challenges and opportunities associated with each season of our life. This involves honesty regarding the challenges ("At this stage in our family's life, it is just not possible for me to get more than a half an hour in solitude a day") and willingness to embrace the opportunities ("Being around small children is teaching me so much about being a child in God's presence"). Our expectations about ordering our life during the different seasons need to take into account what's real and can't be changed; otherwise we set ourselves up for frustration and failure. This is a place for learning how to be compassionate with ourselves, because God certainly is.

An effective rhythm of spiritual practices will also be *balanced* among the disciplines that come easily to us and those that stretch us. For those who are extroverted, the disciplines of solitude and silence will be more of a stretch, but it is a stretch toward wholeness. Introverts may feel that they don't need relationships in community, but nothing could be further from the truth. Without a balanced approach to spiritual disciplines, we run the risk of cultivating a one-sided spirituality that will disintegrate under pressure from the part of us we have left undeveloped.

Without community, the introvert would run the risk of becoming isolated and disconnected from reality. Without solitude, the extrovert would run the risk of becoming shallow and unable to discern the still, small voice of God. Without some structure, the spontaneous, unstructured personality can become undisciplined and unfocused. Without some ability to go with the flow, the highly structured person can become rigid and overly attached to his or her own way of doing things, leaving little room for being surprised by God.

Once we have identified a basic rhythm of spiritual practices, it is important that we enter into it with a great deal of *flexibility*. This does not in any way lessen the depth of our intentionality, but it does help us to avoid becoming rigid and legalistic or even selfish about our rhythms. We need to become as clear as we can about what is optimal for our spiritual life and commit ourselves to it, but then we need to hold it openly during those times when things don't work out exactly as we planned. There will be the morning when we can't have solitude because a child has been sick throughout the night. A crisis at work or with a friend will require our presence and prevent us from leaving work at the exact time we planned. The point is that we know that we have set our intention. We are faithful to it to the best of our ability and to the extent that the day-to-day circumstances of our lives allow.

When we are not able to maintain our disciplines just as we had planned, we can know for sure that God's work is not limited to our spiritual disciplines. He will still find a way to come to us in the midst of our real life on that day. In addition, we should feel free to evaluate our rhythms regularly—especially when we have undergone a major life change—to see if they are still realistic and life giving for us. If not, we are perfectly free to make adjustments with God's guidance. In fact, it is good to take time for "gentle noticing" (rather than critiquing and evaluating!) about every six months, and certainly every time there is a major life change, and to make adjustments rather than becoming rigid in our practices.

✎ A SIMPLE PROCESS FOR CULTIVATING SPIRITUAL RHYTHMS

The process of beginning to cultivate our own rhythm of spiritual practices begins with *attending to our desire,* noticing what words, phrases and prayers seem to most consistently capture our sense of longing for God and for spiritual transformation as we are experiencing it these days. *How bad do I want it? Am I willing to rearrange my life for what my heart most wants?* We then express our willingness to God directly, acknowledging the mystery of spiritual transformation and our powerlessness to bring it about. It is important to know, really *know,* that spiritual transformation at this level is a pure gift as we make ourselves available to God. Otherwise our rhythm of spiritual practices can become nothing more than a spiritual self-help program that is full of human effort.

Then we take time to *listen to our experiences with spiritual practices.* We reflect on our experiences with various spiritual disciplines and invite God to show us which have been most life giving and have resulted in true life change. We take note of those times when it seemed as if God met us in the context of our practices and of the transformation that resulted. We observe which disciplines were most stretching for us as well. *Which spiritual practices and relationships have seemed to be most powerful in meeting the desires of my heart?*

The next step is to *begin developing a plan* based on these reflections. *What am I beginning to understand about my minimum daily/weekly/monthly requirements for ongoing spiritual formation? Which disciplines do I know I need to engage in regularly as a way of offering myself to God steadily and consistently?* We ask God for his guidance in putting together a rhythm of spiritual practices that will meet our desire for life-giving connection with him and authentic spiritual transformation. It's important to give thought to the disciplines practiced in solitude, disciplines related to life in our body and disciplines related to life in community.

We take into account the limits and opportunities of our life stage, our personality, our current circumstances, asking questions such as the following:

- What practices will I seek to engage in on a daily basis? Weekly? Monthly? Yearly?
- Where will I engage in these disciplines?
- What time of the day/week/month/year?
- What have I learned about the significance of community for spiritual transformation through the "journeying together" portions of this process? Where might there be an opportunity or an invitation to enter more deeply into community on the basis of shared spiritual disciplines?
- Are there other activities or practices that are particularly suited to my personality type or spiritual type? How will I incorporate these into the rhythm of my spiritual practices?
- Are certain practices particularly needed based on sins and negative patterns that I am aware of?

Making practical arrangements is part of crafting the plan:

- What schedule changes will I need to make in order to consistently choose these life-giving disciplines?
- What arrangements do I need to make with those I live with in order to make this possible?
- Are there any questions or conversations I need to have with those I work with in order to make this possible?

Once we have crafted a plan that is concrete and specific, we *commit ourselves to it prayerfully out of our desire for God* rather than a sense of duty or obligation. Remember, a personal rule of life is a means of opening ourselves in a consistent manner to God's transforming work in us.

Then we *periodically take time to notice*. As we enter into this new way of living, we can feel free to explore and experiment with our rhythms and make adjustments along the way. After about six months, it's good to take some extended time in God's presence to notice how it is going and whether some larger adjustments need to be made. Every time we go through a major life change (getting married, having children, taking on a new job, retiring, moving, having surgery), we do well to reevaluate so as to make adjustments that are realistic for our new situation.

❧ Fresh Disciplines for a Technological Age

As we become more intentional about living according to our deepest desires, it becomes increasingly important to notice the effects of technology on our mind, our soul and our relationships. The effects of technology are so pervasive and have sneaked up on us in such subtle ways that most of us have little awareness of how deep and far-reaching those effects really are.

I realized the full extent of my own frustration with the intrusiveness of technology one morning as I sat on a flight from San Diego to Chicago. I had just completed several days of speaking and was more than ready to go home. As we prepared for takeoff, a man sitting near me was talking very loudly on his cell phone, obviously trying to nail down one last business transaction before the flight attendant ordered us to turn off all phones. Because the previous several days had been quite full of words and activity, I was longing for some uninterrupted quiet and was irritated that I had to listen to the man's conversation.

In that moment I "saw" my world and what it had been reduced to: the only place of refuge from the overstimulation of our highly technologized life was a speeding bullet thirty thousand feet above the earth! And even that small place of refuge was temporary. I realized that I needed a whole new set of spiritual disciplines to deal with the contemporary reality of encroaching technology.

Technology is not evil; it is how we use technology that determines whether it is a force for good or for ill in our lives. As we seek to cultivate spiritual rhythms, we do well to consider disciplines that correspond to the temptations arising from technology so that we can protect the elements of our lives that we value most. Although there are no cookie-cutter approaches to these disciplines, it's helpful to think about certain times of day and aspects of life in relation to the kinds of technologies that affect us.

In the morning. Early morning is a special time of day, when we are in a more rested and undefended state than we are at any other time. The new day stretches out before us unspoiled and full of potential. If we are getting enough rest, the time when we are waking up and preparing for the day is a time of quiet alertness, openness and receptivity, and even energized creativity. How we choose to spend this time has potential to set the tone of the whole day, and depending on the demands of our life, these may be the only moments we have all day for silence and deep listening to God.

At one time I noticed myself slipping into the habit of turning on the cell phone as soon as I wake up and checking my e-mail before I even had my first cup of coffee. Slowly and imperceptibly, these habits were robbing me of moments that used to be for silence, prayer and being present to God. Since I work primarily in a home office, I was often full-bore into the work of the day before I was even fully awake! More recently I have been establishing a discipline of no technology before 9:00 a.m., choosing instead to preserve that time for quiet preparation for the day ahead. Then when it comes time to engage the world, including the world of technology, I find I am much more grounded in God (rather than frenetic) and much more enlivened in my spirit. Although turning on the cell phone and checking e-mails in the early morning hours continue to be temptations, I keep asking myself, *How do I want greet God in the morning? Do I want to begin the day with technology or with quiet listening?*

In the evening. The way we transition from the working day into the evening hours is also very important, because if we do not really transition, our work can bleed into every nook and cranny of our life. The accessibility of e-mail from any Internet connection and the fact that we now wear pagers and cell phones like clothing intensify the temptation to believe that if we do one more thing, we'll somehow catch up with all that needs doing. On one level (the level of checking tasks off a list) this may be true, but on another level (the level of being human and needing time for rest, leisure and relationship) we just get further and further behind.

Those of us who work away from home can become much more intentional about marking a clear ending to the workday when we shut down computers, work cell phones and pagers. We can use the ride home to review the day and call it done. We can join God in his pattern of working and resting and say, "The work of this day is enough, and it is good." If we work from home, unplugging from certain elements of technology can be a symbolic act of releasing the work of this day to God and being fully present to the gifts of eventide: a shared meal, conversation with family and friends, contributions made to life at home, leisure and rest.

Solitude, silence and sabbath. The intrusion of technology into every nook and cranny of our lives in contemporary culture makes it necessary to be very thoughtful regarding our use of technology on the days we have set aside for solitude, silence and sabbath. When I first started leading retreats more than ten years ago, nobody but doctors and a few others in helping professions carried cell phones or pagers, so we didn't really have to deal with the issue. As time went by, more and more people had these devices, but they didn't usually bring them into a retreat setting. Now it is necessary to prepare people ahead of time for the prospect of turning off technology in order to enter into the quiet, and even then participants experience quite a bit of anxiety about being unreachable. It's as if they really feel that the world can't go on without them, even for a day. People are also bringing computers on retreat, because they journal on their computer. In theory this should work, but it may leave an opening for technology to intrude in ways we don't intend. For true silence, we do better to unplug completely.

Because life in contemporary culture requires us to move at high speeds and to be accessible nearly all the time, we need *more* extended times of solitude in which the RPMs of body, mind and soul can slow down. Most of us really need one day a month in solitude, completely unplugged not only from people but also from computer and phones, to maintain enough inner quiet to hear God and allow him to touch us in the deeper places of our being. It is not expedient, it is never convenient, and it means we are inaccessible to family and colleagues. However, on these days we are completely accessible to God, which in the end is better for everyone around us.

Decisions about the use of technology are highly personal, but our attempts to be more thoughtful and disciplined in this area do offer us hope—hope that we do not have to live at the mercy of forces that are subtle and yet intrusive and all-consuming. As we seek to take control of the effects of technology in our life, we are reclaiming space for our soul and for the things that matter to us most deeply.

By Way of Example

My own rule of life these days is very simple, even though it has taken me years to settle into it with clarity. The exact details do not matter to anyone but me; what matters is that it works for me at this time and that when I am living it I am a better person.

Daily. My daily rhythm includes solitude and silence (with no technology) from 7:00 to 9:00 in the morning. This includes at least a half an hour of being in silence and then moving into prayer with words, reflection on Scripture and the other disciplines we have explored. This time also includes getting dressed and making other preparations for the day and sometimes even a short walk, but doing so quietly and prayerfully rather than allowing other kinds of stimulation. At 9:00 I transition into the workday. Of course I have to maintain some flexibility when I am traveling and speaking.

In the late afternoon or evening, I unplug from work-related technology and transition to evening time by going on a bike ride (when possible) and using that time for the examen. I have one spiritual friend I connect with daily and others with whom I connect with weekly or monthly.

Weekly. My weekly rhythm includes commitment to Sunday as the sabbath for myself and for our family. On this day we disconnect from work and work-related technology; we rest, exercise, cook special food, and enjoy each other and friends, choosing activities that are worshipful and also pleasurable.

Monthly. I try to set aside one day a month for solitude, completely unplugged. I also receive spiritual direction once a month and combine it with my solitude day if possible.

Quarterly/half-yearly. At least once a quarter I enter into some sort of extended retreat with others, usually from the Transforming Center. The prayer rhythms, extended times in solitude and engagement in spiritual community are vitally important for my own spiritual health and well-being.

Yearly. Our family takes a vacation of one to two weeks for rest and recreation. In addition, I also try to engage in some kind of training or guided experience where I receive teaching and guidance that keeps me learning and growing.

These rhythms are so specific to the particularities of my life that I almost hesitate to delineate them. I describe them here not so you will try to duplicate them exactly (please don't!) but so that you will have a glimpse of what a concrete, specific rule of life can be. Let me hasten to add that I am not able to do it this way all the time; sometimes life gets in the way. But it is what I shoot for, and that means I hit the mark much more often than I would if I didn't have my aim clearly in view.

Each of us must find our own way of cultivating a rule of life that fits with our own situation. A busy executive describes his own process of establishing a rule of life this way, "I have struggled to practice a coherent life of the Spirit in the midst of the intense workday pressure of casting vision, leading meetings, making budgets, handling personnel problems and so on. I love times of quiet retreat, but they are not my real world. Consequently I have chosen to develop a 'rule of life' that gives me some reference points for living a more spiritual life in the warp and woof of my job as well. Some aspects of this rule are tangible external disciplines like having a daily devotional time. But others are internal disciplines of the heart and mind that are becoming more a part of my lived out life. My rule is a spiritual reminder of my calling and is based on the Great Commandments." As another example, here is his rule.

Cultivating and ordering the affections of the heart
- having a "quiet heart" that is not distraught with internal regrets nor frenzied by external circumstances
- having a "circumcised heart" that is cut free from having to be right and is free from attachments to sports, food, recognition from others
- having a "burning heart" that is focused on pleasing God
- having a "dancing heart" that serves others with joy and gladness

Nurturing the inclinations of my soul
- having a daily "quiet time" for Bible reading and prayer
- having a weekly sabbath for corporate worship and rest and praying through my rule of life
- being part of Christian community in my local church
- taking quarterly retreats for more extended reflection and recalibration of my rule of life

Strengthening the disciplines and illumination of my mind
- pursuing a "humble mind" that honors unity over victory

- desiring a "renewed mind" that resists conformity to the world for the sake of spiritual transformation
- developing a "prepared mind" for understanding and living my faith

Practicing the habits of my strength

- daily stewardship
    - maintain a minimum of seven hours of sleep a night
    - thirty-minute quiet time resting in assurance of God's love
    - vigorous exercise three times a week
    - healthy diet
    - no evening television without my wife
- stewardship of gifts of study
    - reading in areas of history and culture
- stewardship of vocational calling
    - being involved and attentive to others: listening, learning and loving them
    - investing in others: taking time to teach and touch others with grace
    - inspiring others with vision, encouragement and empowerment

Loving my neighbor as myself

- being friendly with neighbors
- being compassionate to those in need
- seeking justice and mercy in the world
- being an agent of reconciliation: making all things new rather than all new things
- being a person of engagement and not avoidance

He concludes by saying, "I do not 'obey' my rule as with an arbitrary checklist, but I do allow it to shape my daily life through the promptings of the Holy Spirit."

⚜ THE POWER OF COMMUNITY FOR SPIRITUAL TRANSFORMATION

It is impossible to overstate the importance of community in the spiritual transformation process. This is not the same thing as the Christian busyness that often accompanies church life; it is about quietly sharing the journey with others who are also drawn to deeper levels of spiritual transformation that enable them to discern and do God's will. As noted earlier, Jesus chose a spiritual community to accompany him on his spiritual journey on this earth, and he defined his spiritual community as those who were willing to seek out and do the will of God (Mark 3:33-34).

The desire to know and do the will of God and to live a life that made this possible formed the disciples' primary identity, and it was on this basis that they came together in unity. They ate together, traveled together, slept out under the stars together, ministered together, talked, asked questions, argued and challenged each other. They stayed together under duress, conflict, betrayal and even death, seeking to do the will of God and to become more like Jesus in the process. In the crucible of community they were shaped and molded to become the future leaders of the church. They were changed as individuals, and ultimately they changed the world through the inauguration of a new kind of relationship with God through the person of Christ.

Taking a closer look at the relational rhythm of Jesus' life, we notice that within the small group of twelve there were three disciples with whom he was especially intimate. These three he invited to be with him in his most private moments of grief and agitation in the Garden of Gethsemane. Even though they failed him significantly then, Jesus' request to them show that he was in touch with his need for intimate friendship and spiritual support. It is one thing to tell someone about something that you have wrestled with and overcome in the past tense; it is quite another to invite someone to be with you in your current struggle when you aren't sure of the outcome! Relationship at this level is truly transforming.

Within the larger community of faith there are a select few with whom we can feel safe enough to move more deeply into confession, truth telling, asking penetrating questions, challenging and confronting one another, giving and receiving spiritual guidance. In Christian tradition, this kind of relationship is called spiritual friendship. Such relationships are characterized by a spark of affinity that over time deepens into love. They are characterized by each person's profound willingness to be known by the other. As that love grows, a level of challenge is accepted and even expected because there is deep commitment to each other's well-being.

As you conclude your initial work with your spiritual rhythms, it is of utmost importance that you realize that you cannot do this alone. None of us can. Within your commitment to the larger faith community, the church, seek to identify at least one other person, if not several, who shares your desire for God and is willing to walk the path of establishing spiritual rhythms with you. "Two are better than one. . . . For if they fall, one will lift up the other; but woe to one who is alone and falls and does not have another to help" (Ecclesiastes 4:9-10).

The path to spiritual wholeness lies in my increasingly faithful response to the One whose purpose shapes my path, whose power liberates me from the crippling bondages of my previous journey, and whose transforming presence meets me at every turn in the road.

ROBERT MULHOLLAND,
INVITATION TO A JOURNEY

⧈ SACRED DESIRE, SACRED RHYTHMS

Desire has its own rhythms. Sometimes it ebbs and sometimes it flows. But in the end it is the deepening of spiritual desire and the discipline to arrange our life around our desire that carries us from the shallow waters of superficial human wanting into our soul's movement in the very depths of God. Sometimes the tide brings us closer in to the shore and the soul frolics in the waves. But increasingly we find our life to be hidden in the depths of God, and whatever is seen on the surface springs up from those depths full of beauty and grace.

I don't know about you, but I yearn for the freedom and beauty of a life that is completely oriented to the reality of God. I long to experience my soul hidden and content in the very depths of God, so that what is seen on the surface is transformed and energized by what takes place in those depths. The choice to orient our life to God's transforming presence is always ours; sacred rhythms help us to say yes to this desire, day by day by day.

> Ask me not where I live
> or what I like to eat. . . .
> Ask me what I am living for
> and what I think is keeping me
> from living fully for that.
> THOMAS MERTON, *Thoughts in Solitude*

〰️ PRACTICE

As you come to the end of this book, schedule some retreat time or some extended solitude at home to reflect on your experiences with the spiritual disciplines you have explored. As you begin your reflection, take time to enter into the kind of quiet that enables your soul to come out in God's presence.

Attend to your desire. Ask: What words, phrases, prayers seem to most consistently capture my sense of longing for God and for spiritual transformation as I am experiencing it these days? What do I sense is most needed these days?

Acknowledge the mystery of spiritual transformation and your pow-

erlessness to bring it about. Ask: In what area(s) of my life right now am I most aware of my need for transformation and my powerlessness to bring it about? Acknowledge your powerlessness to God, and tell him of your desire to make yourself available to him in a consistent way so that he can do his transforming work in you.

Listen to your experiences with spiritual practices. Invite God to show you which disciplines practiced in which ways have been most life giving to you. Notice points of consolation and desolation as well as times when it seemed as if God met you in the context of your practices. Notice which ones have been most stretching and which ones are resulting in deeper levels of connection with God and transformation toward Christlikeness. Ask: Which spiritual practices and relationships seem to be most powerful in fulfilling the desires of my heart right now?

Begin developing a plan. Based on your reflections, what are you beginning to understand about your minimum daily/weekly/monthly requirements for ongoing spiritual formation? What you have observed? What concrete activities do you want to engage in as ways of offering yourself to God steadily and consistently? Ask God for his guidance in putting together a rhythm of spiritual practices that will meet your desire for life-giving connection with him and authentic spiritual transformation.

- solitude and silence (daily and extended)
- prayer
- *lectio divina*
- examen of consciousness
- self-examination and confession
- honoring the body
- discernment (consolation and desolation)
- sabbath
- community

Write out your plan. Be sure to take into account the limits and opportunities of your life stage, your personality, your circumstances.

1. What practices will I seek to engage in on a daily basis? Weekly? Monthly? Yearly? Where will I engage in these disciplines? What time of the day/week/month/year?

2. In the "journeying together" process, what have I learned about the importance of community?

   What spiritual disciplines will I share with a spiritual friend, or a group of friends, so as to grow together?

3. What additional activities or practices are particularly important given my personality type or spiritual type?

   How will I incorporate these into the rhythm of my spiritual practices?

   Are there practices that are particularly needed because of my sins and negative patterns? (See appendix A, which lists various sins and the disciplines that can help address them.)

4. How will I need to adjust my schedule in order to consistently choose this rule of life?

What arrangements do I need to make with those I live with?

Do I need to have any discussions with those I work with in order to make this possible?

Take a break. After you have captured in writing your desire and plan for establishing spiritual rhythms, take a break if you wish. Go for a walk, take a nap, do some reading, pray or sit in silence. If you are spending time on this at home, feel free to set it aside for a day or two. Then come back to it and take another look at your plan.

How does it look and feel to you now? Is it personal enough? Balanced? Realistic?

Are you able to think of it as a flexible undertaking rather than a legalistic straitjacket?

Are there any questions or concerns that you would like to raise with your spiritual friend or others who can pray for you?

Commit yourself prayerfully. Are you able to commit yourself to this plan *out of desire for God* rather than a sense of obligation?

As you feel ready, commit yourself prayerfully to your personal rule of life as a means of releasing yourself in a consistent manner to God's transforming work in you.

Notice gently. Feel free to explore and experiment with your rhythms and make adjustments along the way. After about six months, take some extended time in God's presence to evaluate how it is going and decide whether any larger adjustments need to be made.

A Note of Gratitude

"The older you get, the gentler and kinder the Mystery seems."

A DEVOUT NINETY-FOUR YEAR OLD WOMAN

I have a confession to make. Toward the end of the writing of this book, I lost my rhythms. For various reasons, I struggled to get the manuscript in on time, and as the deadline loomed, I had to radically reorient my life toward finishing this project. Without going into all the gory details, it is enough to admit that it happened—just like it happens to all of us from time to time—and to tell you what I discovered during that time.

From the vantage point of being outside my normal rhythms for a time, I saw my life more clearly than I sometimes do. I became deeply aware of the fact that I love my life when I am living it within the rhythms that God has guided me into; there is a goodness in it and manageability to it that my whole self longs for and leans into. Yes, there is busyness and work, but there are also times of rest and delight that my soul can count on. There are the normal pains and challenges of life, but there is also the everyday beauty and fullness that comes from paying attention and finding God in the midst of it all.

As I worked my way through those long weeks (and thank God it was only a few weeks!), I found myself saying, "I don't want to write about rhythms anymore; I just want to live them!" In the midst of struggling to get it all into words, it was good to know—really *know*—that the wisdom contained in the Christian tradition of cultivating a rule of life really is true. It is not merely another self-help plan; it is a way of living our lives in God that is meant for the fulfillment of our deepest longings—as much as is possible this side of heaven. It is meant to lead us into a way of life that works in the deepest ways.

And so I am full of gratitude for the kindness and the gentleness of the Mystery who does not judge or berate but gently woos us back to that which is good. And I am grateful for family, friends and publishing colleagues who have been patient and caring, praying and loving me along until the work was finished. It is my prayer for all of us that we will find our way into those life rhythms that cause us to love our lives, not because they are perfect but because we are experiencing God with us and are arranging our lives for what our hearts want most.

APPENDIX A

Journeying Together

The purpose of journeying together in spiritual friendship and spiritual community (whether there are just two of you or whether you are in a small group) is to listen to one another's desire for God, to nurture that desire in each other and to support one another in seeking a way of life that is consistent with that desire. Spiritual friendship is not for advice giving, problem solving and fixing. It's not even about Bible study. Rather it is to assist one another in paying attention to the movements of God in our lives through the spiritual disciplines and to support another in responding faithfully to God's presence.

The best way to experience this book together is to move chapter by chapter. Each person reads the chapter ahead of time and practices the discipline personally. Then when you come together, you can reflect on your experiences together and also enter into some aspect of the discipline together. If you are leading the group, you'll find some further suggestions in appendix B.

✑ CHAPTER 1: LONGING FOR MORE

Begin with a few moments of silence, creating space for each of you to settle into a stance of quiet listening to God and of preparation for listening deeply to one another. In the quiet, reflect on your experience of listening to your longings and what you feel God is inviting you to make known to the group. After several moments of silence, the leader or a designated person can offer a brief prayer, asking God to guide your time together and to help you truly listen to each other.

Invite each person to share their experience of attending to desire in God's presence using the following questions.

Where did you see yourself most clearly in the various stories where Jesus asked, "What do you want me to do for you?" (Some people may not have even gotten to the point where they could hear Jesus ask them the question. They may still be experiencing themselves sitting by the side of the road or lying by the pool. This is fine. Allow people to be right where they are in the story and describe their experience.)

How did you respond to Jesus' question as you heard him address you personally? What are the feelings and the words that express your desire as you are experiencing it these days? (Encourage people to share from their journal if that is helpful to them.)

How did you experience God's response to you in the midst of your desire? (Desire is a very tender, vulnerable thing to talk about with others. Be very careful to receive each person's words reverently and with gratitude. Be supportive but also be careful not to rush in with your own thoughts and perspectives.)

Close your time together in prayer, thanking God for his presence with you. If you wish, go around the circle and have each person pray for the person on their right, affirming their desire and asking God to continue to meet them in the midst of it. If there is any action step that they feel called to, pray that God would give them the courage to take that step.

⚞ CHAPTER 2: SOLITUDE

Begin with a few moments of silence to remind yourselves of your purpose for meeting together and to transition from chatting and catching up to a place of deeper listening to each other. If you have time, the silence could involve fifteen minutes to half an hour for participants to experience the practice at the end of the chapter. Designate one person to close the time of silence with a prayer of invitation for God to guide you and assist you in being companions for one another.

Tell each other about your experiences with solitude and silence, remembering that there are no "right" or "wrong" answers, since silence is our invitation to God to speak and move within us *at his own initiative.* Part of the discipline consists of beginning to release our control mechanisms and create space for receiving whatever God gives (or doesn't give) in these moments.

What has it been like for you to sit quietly, to rest in God and allow your soul to come out? Has your soul had something to say that it hadn't been able to say in the noisy and busyness of your life? Is there anything God has finally been able to say to you in the quiet?

Is there anything in particular that seemed to hinder your attempts to honor this commitment? How has God been guiding you in this?

What are your plans for becoming more intentional about incorporating soli-tude and silence into the rhythm of your ordinary life? Have you been able to identify a "sacred space"—a time and place that is set apart for God and God alone?

Are you entering in out of desire rather than feeling like it's one more thing you have to do?

At the end of your time together, take time to pray very simply for one another that God would help you in your attempts to establish a rhythm of solitude.

⪘ CHAPTER 3: SCRIPTURE

Begin your time together with silence and then a brief prayer, asking God to help you listen to him and to each other in the midst of your gathering.

You may want to then ask a general question, "How is it with your soul?" giving ample time and space for each person to open up to the depth that is comfortable for them before moving to the specific topic of Scripture.

Summarize your response to this chapter's distinctions between reading a text-book and reading a love letter. What has your approach to Scripture been lately—more like reading a textbook or reading a love letter?

Next you will actually enter into the *lectio* process as a group exercise and then debrief it together. Have the group leader or a designated person lead the process, following the moves in the *lectio* process but giving time for group members to share what God is saying to them as you go through it. If there is a passage you would like to use for this exercise, go ahead and use that. If not, use Mark 10:48-52.

Preparation. Take a moment to become fully present. Let your body relax, and allow yourself to become consciously aware of God's presence with you. Breathe deeply. Express your desire to hear from God, using a brief prayer such as "Come Lord Jesus" or "Here I am" or "Speak, Lord, for your servant is listening."

Read: Listen for the word or the phrase that strikes you. The leader reminds the group, "Listen for the word or phrase that strikes you or catches your attention," and then reads Mark 10:48-52 slowly, pausing between phrases and sentences. After the reading, the leader allows a moment of silence in which individuals can ponder and savor the word that has been given to them without judging or analyzing it. After the silence, the leader invites participants to go around the circle and speak the word they have received, with no discussion and no commentary. Anyone can feel free to say "I pass" if they wish.

Reflect: How is my life touched by this word? Reminding the group that this time they are to listen for the way the passage connects with their life, the leader reads the passage again. Allow several moments of silence following this reading to explore thoughts, perceptions and sensory impressions. If the passage is a story, each person can ask silently, *Where am I in this story? What do I hear as I imagine myself in the story or hear these words addressed specifically to me?* The leader then invites participants to go around the circle and say briefly how their life is touched by this word.

Respond: Is there an invitation for me to respond in some way? The leader reads the passage one more time, inviting group members to listen for God's invitation to them. In the silence that follows the reading, they may respond to God's invitation, allowing their prayer to flow from the heart as fully and as truly as they can, entering into a dialogue with God. After a minute or two of silence, the leader invites participants to go around and state what they sense is God's invitation to them. Again, do not elaborate, explain, justify or comment on what each other is saying. Just receive it with a prayerful spirit.

Rest: Rest in the Word of God. The leader reads the passage one last time, this time inviting group members to release any concerns they might have and return to a place of rest in God. In the silence that follows, rest in God's presence like the weaned child who leans against its mother in a posture of total yieldedness. After a minute or two of silence, the leader can close with a brief prayer, or you can pray around the circle by having each person pray briefly for the person on their right.

A few more questions can help the group process their *lectio divina* experiences so far.

What aspects of the lectio divina process are comfortable for you? Which aspects are uncomfortable?

What have you been hearing from God these days through the Scriptures? Is there a specific word you have been given?

What are God's invitations to you? How are you responding?

Be careful not to "talk it to death." Allow people to leave quietly so they do not lose the impact of what God has said to them.

≫ CHAPTER 4: PRAYER

Begin with a few moments of silence and a prayer of invitation for God to guide your sharing. Then talk to each other about what prayer is like for you these days.

Do you sense that you are in the transitional place that this chapter describes? Do you have a sense that God is inviting you into intimacy with him that is beyond words?

What has it been like for you to sit in stillness and begin to listen for your breath prayer? Tell each other as little or as much as you wish about your breath prayer. (Do not coerce anyone to do this, as the breath prayer is very intimate.)

If you are meeting with one spiritual friend, take time to pray for one another using the following exercise. If you are meeting in a small group, pair up to do this exercise. It is important that you find a quiet place where you will not be distracted or interrupted.

One of you will choose to go first and one of you will go second, allotting about fifteen minutes for each person. Move through the entire exercise for one person and then for the other.

Silence. Begin your time of prayer with a few moments of silence in which you identify and find words to ask God for what you are most needing and wanting from God right now. This does not have to be anything major or earth shattering, just something that you are concerned about. During this time your spiritual friend will sit quietly with you, supporting you with care and silent prayer.

Supplication. When you feel ready, briefly tell your friend what you are understanding about your spiritual desire, and let him or her know your breath prayer if that feels appropriate. Then express this desire out loud to God in prayer.

Intercession. When you are finished praying aloud, your spiritual friend will pray for you, perhaps reiterating what they heard you say regarding your desire, validating it, interceding on your behalf.

Rest. When there are no more words, spend another moment in silence, resting together in your knowledge of God's good intent toward you and his infinite capacity to carry it out. You may wish to end this time with a simple expression of gratitude to your friend for praying with you and for you.

Repeat this process for the other person. As you leave one another's company, commit yourselves to continue to intercede for one another throughout the week.

CHAPTER 5: HONORING THE BODY

Begin your time together by taking time to be silent and to breathe. Pay particular attention to your posture and the comfort of your body. Breathe deeply at least three times and then rest comfortably in your chair for a few moments. Designate someone to close the silent time with prayer, inviting God's presence as you share.

Reflect together on your experience of life in a body.

How easy or how difficult is it for you to think of honoring the body as a spiritual discipline?

In your reading and in your practice, where has God been speaking most clearly about honoring your body as a part of your life in him?

Do you need to care for your body more intentionally? What will that involve for you?

Is there something your body has been trying to tell you that you have not been listening to? How are you responding to this awareness?

How has your body been guiding you to pray? How have you responded? Is there any way you might connect your life in the body with your spiritual practices?

As a part of your small group experience, you might take time to go for a slow, meditative walk together or even do something as simple as kneeling together as you pray.

CHAPTER 6: SELF-EXAMINATION

Take five minutes at the beginning of your time together to sit in silence and enter into the prayer of examen as you have learned it in this chapter. In the silence, reflect on the last twenty-four hours.

Notice those places where God was present and the places where he seemed absent. Notice those places where you experienced the goodness of your created self and the ways God is transforming you. Thank God for his goodness in your life. Also, notice those places where you were not all that you would like to be, times when you were not like Christ. Without judging and berating yourself, allow God to show you what contributed to the situation. Confess to him, if you are ready to do so. Allow yourself to receive his forgiveness.

After five minutes or so, the leader (or someone the group has designated) can bring the silence to a close by offering a brief prayer. Move into a time of reflection, telling one another about your experience of incorporating the examen of consciousness and the examen of conscience into your spiritual rhythms.

When has it worked well for you to carry out this practice?

As you have practiced this way of reviewing your days, what have you noticed about God's presence with you? Were there ways God was with you that you would not have noticed if you had not been practicing this discipline?

Were there places where God's presence surprised you, places where you did not expect him?

Are there aspects of your created self that you have been able to celebrate and acknowledge as being deeply good? What difference has that made?

Are there sins or negative patterns that God has shown you in your times of examen? How is it changing you to acknowledge these areas to God and to those who have been affected by these attitudes and behaviors? Have you been able to move through the self-examination process to confession, release and forgiveness?

Is there a way the group can support and pray for you in your practice of self-examination?

〰️ Chapter 7: Discernment

With your spiritual friend or small group community, spend some time reflecting on the idea that God's will is generally for us to do more of whatever it is that gives us life (Deuteronomy 30:19; John 10:10). How has this changed the way you are looking at your life?

Enter into a time of silence (3-5 minutes) in order to reflect privately on your recent experiences with consolation and desolation using the following questions:

Since the group was last together, when have you had a sense of life-giving connection with God, an ability to be your most authentic self in God and to bring that authentic self to others in love?

When did you have a sense of being cut off from a life-giving connection with God, from the ability to be your authentic self and give yourself to others in love?

After the silence, invite members to share their experiences of consolation and desolation.

What wisdom, insight or further questions seem to arise from this awareness?

How might God be inviting you to incorporate into your life more of that which gives you life and less of that which drains life from you?

The following discussion is optional; you may wish to save it until the next time you are together.

Is anyone in the group facing a decision and sensing a strong desire to know God's will and enter into the practice of discernment? Invite them to talk about the decision they are facing, and then ask the following questions.

Where are you in the process of discernment as it is outlined in this chapter (prayer for indifference, prayer for wisdom, noticing without judging, gathering data)?

What are the things that are clear to you right now? What are your questions?

What do you need from God and from others as you seek to make this decision?

Take time to pray for those who are seeking God's wisdom in this way. If several members of the group are facing decisions and seeking to implement the practice of discernment, consider giving a whole session to this.

∞ CHAPTER 8: SABBATH

Begin your time together by having someone in the group read pages 143-44, beginning with "There have to be times in your life when you move slow . . . times when you walk rather than run . . ." Read to the end of the chapter, and take a few moments in silence to allow group members to reflect on their need and their longing for such fullness of time. Draw the silence to a close by offering a brief prayer of invitation to God to help you to live into your longings.

Talk to each other about where you are on the journey of exploring a sabbath practice.

Where are the places in your life where you are experiencing human limitations? When are you aware of your own desire for a sane rhythm of work and rest? Did any experiences that the author describes in this chapter particularly resonate with you?

Where are you in terms of motivation to begin incorporating sabbath time into your life? What are the challenges and impossibilities particular to your situation? Where do you think it might be possible for you to, at least, make a beginning?

Have you already been practicing the discipline of sabbath keeping? Is there anything you can share from your real life experience that might be helpful to the group?

End your time together by inviting each person to state their desire and intent regarding sabbath. If there is even one small step they can take toward practicing a sabbath, they should state that as well. Pray for one another that God would enable each one to take the step, no matter how small, that they have identified.

CHAPTER 9: A RULE OF LIFE

Begin your time together with a few moments of silence in which you give yourselves space to reflect on your longing for a way of life that works, a way of life that enables you to make daily choices to enter more deeply into the process of spiritual transformation.

What is the longing of your heart these days? When do you feel your longing? What does your longing say to you?

After a few moments of silence, have the leader or a designated person speak out a brief prayer of invitation to God to guide you as you share your lives by responding to the following questions.

How has your desire deepened into greater intentionality regarding spiritual practices over the last months?

Which disciplines have been most meaningful in producing the kind of life change you are seeking? What difference has it made to start incorporating these disciplines into your life?

As you have worked with the "Practice" exercises, how are you doing with putting together a rhythm of spiritual practices that enables you to live consistently with your heart's deepest longings?

What are your MDR (minimum daily requirements) for maintaining the intimacy and availability to God that result in spiritual transformation? What are the daily, weekly, monthly rhythms that you would like to commit yourself to as a way to begin?

What arrangements do you need to make with those closest to you?

What challenges do you anticipate?

How will you continue to maintain spiritual friendship or spiritual community that helps you to live consistently with your heart's desire and continue to notice and respond to God's transforming work in your life?

After each person explains the rhythms they are seeking to establish, pray for God to enable them to press through any challenges that face them so that they can respond with increasing faithfulness to God's invitations.

APPENDIX B

Leading a Group Experience

It is important to begin your group's shared exploration of *Sacred Rhythms* by clarifying the purpose of the group. The small group gathers to listen to one another's desire for God, to support one another in the spiritual practices that help us to seek God, and to assist one another in paying attention to the activity of God in our everyday lives and in our spiritual practices.

After clarifying the group's purpose, ask group members if they are indeed willing to journey together as a small community in order to nurture one another's desire for God and to support one another in seeking a way of life that is consistent with that desire. If the answer is yes, guide the group in making the following basic commitments as they journey together (if needed, encourage them to add any other values or commitments that will increase their sense of willingness to commit themselves to the group):

- We will be faithful to our own personal rhythm of spiritual practices.

- We will support and pray for one another as we each seek to cultivate a rhythm of spiritual practices in our own lives and respond faithfully to God's invitations along the way.

- We will respect each other's personal relationship with God understanding that each person's relationship with God takes place *at God's initiative* and within his leading and control.

- We will create and maintain a safe environment for questions and wondering. This means we will listen rather than fix and ask questions rather than give answers.

- We will seek to increase our self-awareness and be appropriately self-disclosing.
- We will pay particular attention to the times and ways in which God is moving in each person's life and seek to affirm evidence of each person's growth and transformation.
- We will honor confidentiality. What is shared in the group stays in the group!

You as the leader will need to model these values and behaviors for the group and, at times, you may need to remind the group about this way of being together—especially in the early stages of the group's development. Sometimes you may need to guide the group back if it begins to digress into mere discussion of ideas, advice-giving, problem-solving or sharing information. Remember that the focus is on transformation, not information.

As much as possible, follow the suggestions for incorporating aspects of the disciplines into your times together. The discipline of beginning with shared silence, in particular, is one that prepares the group to be together in meaningful ways rather than allowing the time to degenerate into small talk and surface conversation. Although it may feel uncomfortable at first, you will serve the group best by helping them to actually experience the disciplines together. Closing your time with prayer that celebrates what God is doing in each person's life and affirms each person's spiritual desire and intent for the week to come is an important way of "gathering up" all that has been shared and entrusting it to God.

In the end, the most important thing you can do as a leader is to be faithful to your own exploration of the practices so that you are able to share and offer perspective that can only come from your own experience. Be sure to share your successes and your struggles as a fellow traveler on the journey of spiritual transformation.

APPENDIX C

Choosing Spiritual Disciplines that Correspond to Our Needs

One way to become more intentional about our spiritual rhythms is to choose spiritual practices and relationships appropriate to the particular sins and negative patterns that God is helping us become aware of. While the spiritual disciplines explored in this book are all considered to be basic to the Christian life, there are times when certain disciplines can be entered into with greater emphasis because they are particularly effective in allowing God to work with us in specific areas where we know we are not like Christ. For instance, those who struggle with sins of speech will benefit from an emphasis on the discipline of silence even though it will probably be very challenging for them. Those who wrestle with negative thought patterns will want to spend more time allowing the Scriptures to wash over them during *lectio divina*.

Our arrangement of spiritual practices and relationships becomes more personal as we choose disciplines that correspond to those areas where we recognize our specific need for spiritual transformation. The following list is not an exhaustive one in that it deals only with the disciplines mentioned in this book, and it is only representative of different sin patterns that exist in us as human beings. (For a more exhaustive list of spiritual disciplines, see Adele Calhoun, *Spiritual Disciplines Handbook*, InterVarsity Press.) However, it is a place to start in identifying those spiritual disciplines that are most important for you at this time;

as you continue to explore the disciplines, you will begin to have your own experiences of which disciplines are effective for the different patterns you are becoming aware of.

The following list offers a few examples to help you begin looking at the disciplines in this way. After identifying one or two areas where you are aware of your need for transformation, you can then begin incorporating the corresponding disciplines into your life much more intentionally. In the words of Richard Foster, "These disciplines are the main way we offer our bodies up to God as a living sacrifice. We are doing what we can do with our bodies, our minds, our hearts. God then takes this simple offering of ourselves and does with it what we cannot do, producing within us deeply ingrained habits of love and peace and joy in the Holy Spirit."

Sins and Negative Patterns	Corresponding Disciplines
Gossip/sins of speech	Silence, self-examination
Anxiety and worry	Breath prayer, Scripture reflection
Envy and competitiveness	Solitude, self-examination
Discontent	Attending to desire
Self-reliance	Silence, prayer, community
Avoidance patterns	Community, spiritual friendship
Over-busyness	Solitude, discernment, sabbath, rule of life
Anger and bitterness	Silence, self-examination, confession
Feelings of inadequacy	Examen of consciousness, self-knowledge and celebration
Guilt, shame	Solitude, confession, forgiveness
Lust	Attending to desire in God's presence
Restlessness and stress	Solitude, silence, breath prayer
Lethargy and/or laziness	Caring for the body, exercise
Lack of faith	Prayer, Scripture
Feelings of isolation	Examen of consciousness, community
Selfishness and self-centeredness	Prayer and worship in community
Lack of direction	Discernment, listening to the body

You begin to get the idea . . .

Notes

Introduction

pp. 13-14 "What shapes our actions": Ronald Rolheiser, *The Holy Longing* (New York: Doubleday, 1999), p. 7.

Chapter 1: Longing for More

p. 23 Examples of Jesus' questions "What do you want? What do you want me to do for you?" can be found in Matthew 20:20-23, 29-34; Mark 10:35-40, 46-52; John 5:6-7.

Chapter 2: Solitude

pp. 33-34 The story of the priest and the woman comes from Anthony DeMello, *Taking Flight* (New York: Doubleday, 1988), p. 29.

p. 41 "A book that chronicled my own journey": Ruth Haley Barton, *Invitation to Solitude and Silence* (Downers Grove, Ill.: InterVarsity Press, 2004).

Chapter 3: Scripture

pp. 48-50 Discussion of reading for information versus formation: I am indebted to Robert Mulholland for his perspective on distinguishing between reading for information and reading for formation in *Shaped by the Word* (Nashville: Upper Room, 1985).

p. 52 Cognitive, rational functions "are so hyper-developed in our culture": M. Robert Mulholland, *Shaped by the Word*, p. 23.

pp. 56-58 The four movements of *lectio divina:* This approach to Scripture is so old that it was originally presented in Latin. Although I have chosen English words to name the movements in the process, I have included the Latin words in parentheses so that the beauty and the nuance of the original language is not lost.

p. 60   "Sharing with God the feelings": Mulholland, *Shaped by the Word*, p. 114.

Chapter 4: Prayer

p. 63   "Words pour out to begin with": Carlo Carretto, *Letters from the Desert* (Maryknoll, N.Y.: Orbis, 1972), p. 40.

p. 66   "When we read God's story": Henri J. M. Nouwen, "Running from What We Desire," *Partnership,* July/August 1986, p. 34.

p. 68   *"Be still before the Lord and wait"*: Psalm 37:7; Psalm 46:10; Psalm 62:1.

p. 70   "In this period, the so-called litanical prayer thrives": Carretto, *Letters from the Desert*, p. 43.

p. 76   "There are several components to this practice": I am deeply indebted to Joe Sherman, cofounder of the Transforming Center and liturgist, for his guidance in developing the prayer rhythms of the Transforming Center.

Chapter 5: Honoring the Body

p. 81   "An ambiguous legacy": Stephanie Paulsell in *Practicing Our Faith* (San Francisco: Jossey-Bass, 1977), p. 16.

p. 83   "Our sexual feelings intensify as we are made whole": Flora Slossun Wuellner, *Prayer and Our Bodies* (Nashville: Upper Room, 1987), p. 71.

p. 84   "A biological mechanism is at work": William C. Bushell quoted in Ira Dreyfuss, "Exercise Boosts Spirituality," *Daily Herald*.

p. 85   "My body, once ignored and despised, has become an ally": Elouise Renich Fraser, *Confessions of a Beginning Theologian* (Downers Grove, Ill.: InterVarsity Press, 1998), p. 31.

p. 87   "Praying with all of who we are": Jane E. Vennard, *Praying with Body and Soul: A Way to Intimacy with God* (Minneapolis: Augsburg, 1998), p. 5.

Chapter 6: Self-Examination

pp. 92-93 "Our cross is the point of our unlikeness": M. Robert Mulholland (Downers Grove, Ill.: InterVarsity Press, 1993), *Invitation to a Journey*, p. 38.

p. 102   Discussion of purgation: The language of purgation hearkens back to David's request of God in Psalm 51, where he says, "Purge me with hyssop and I will be clean."

pp. 102-3   Robert Mulholland characterizes the layers of purgation in Mulholland, *Invitation to a Journey,* pp. 82-86.

Chapter 7: Discernment

p. 117   We are "quite certain that there is no 'catch'": Dallas Willard, *The Divine Conspiracy* (New York: HarperSanFrancisco, 1998), p. 321.

p. 118   The Holy Spirit expands Christ's teaching: see Thomas Hart, *The Art of Christian Listening* (New York: Paulist, 1980), p. 67.

p. 119   "God's will, nothing more": Danny Morris and Chuck Olsen, *Discerning God's Will Together* (Nashville: Upper Room Books, 1997), p. 90.

p. 120   "The question that is most pertinent": Morris and Olsen, *Discerning God's Will,* p. 76.

p. 120   "The first call of the Gospel, says Teilhard de Chardin": Ernest Larkin, *Silent Presence* (Denville, N.J.: Dimension, 1981), p. 13.

pp. 121-22   "Deep within us all there is an amazing inner sanctuary": Thomas Kelly, *A Testament of Devotion* (New York: Harper & Row, 1969), p. 3.

p. 123   "Wants are mine; shoulds are someone else's": Hart, *Art of Christian Listening,* p. 77.

p. 126   "Depends greatly on our spiritual and psychological maturity": Larkin, *Silent Presence,* p. 59.

p. 127   "Nothing is more practical than finding God": Pedro Arrupe, S.J. (1907-1991), 28th General of the Society of Jesus (1965-1981) <www.calprov.org/vocations/vocationsreflections.html>.

p. 127   Discernment exercise: adapted from Dennis Linn, Sheila Fabricant Linn and Matthew Linn, *Sleeping with Bread: Holding What Gives You Life* (Mahwan, N.Y.: Paulist, 1995), pp. 5-9.

Chapter 8: Sabbath

p. 131   "If we do not allow for a rhythm of rest": Wayne Muller, *Sabbath* (New York: Bantam, 1999), p. 1.

p. 135   "It was as if a whole people were in love with the seventh day": Abraham Heschel, *The Sabbath* (New York: Farrar, Straus & Giroux, 1951), pp. 15-17.

p. 136   The contrast between Jewish Shabbat and Sunday afternoon at the Mudhouse coffee shop comes from Lauren Winner, *Mudhouse Sabbath* (Brewster, Miss.: Paraclete, 2003), pp. 3-4.

p. 139   "Because we do not rest": Muller, *Sabbath.*

Chapter 9: A Rule of Life

p. 147   If you are interested in exploring St. Benedict's Rule more carefully, an
           excellent translation is *The Rule of St. Benedict in English,* ed. Timothy Fry
           OSB (Collegeville, Minn.: Liturgical Press, 1982). In addition, there are
           many commentaries and applications of St. Benedict's Rule for modern
           life. Two that I have appreciated most are Esther de Waal's *Living with
           Contradiction: An Introduction to Benedictine Spirituality* (Harrisburg,
           Penn.: Morehouse Publishing, 1997), and Brian C. Taylor's *Spirituality
           for Everyday Living: An Adaptation of the Rule of St. Benedict* (Collegeville,
           Minn.: Liturgical Press, 1989).

p. 148   Other resources that would be very helpful for you as you develop your
           own rule of life are *Soulfeast: An Invitation to the Christian Spiritual Life* by
           Marjorie Thompson (Nashville: Upper Room, 1995), and *Practicing Our
           Faith: A Way of Life for Searching People,* ed. Dorothy Bass (San Francisco:
           Jossey-Bass, 1997).

Appendix C: Choosing Spiritual Disciplines that Correspond to Our Needs

p. 187   "These disciplines are the main way": Richard Foster, "Growing Edges,"
           Perspective 9, no. 2 (April 1999), p.1.

TRANSFORMING CENTER
Strengthening the Soul of Your Leadership

Resources to Help You Experience Spiritual Transformation

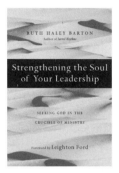

Strengthening the Soul of Your Leadership

ISBN 978-0-8308-3513-3

Longing for More

ISBN 978-0-8308-3506-5

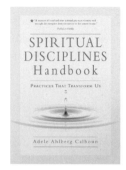

Spiritual Disciplines Handbook

ISBN 978-0-8308-3330-6

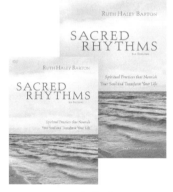

Sacred Rhythms
DVD and Participant's Guide

video download also available,
all from www.Zondervan.com

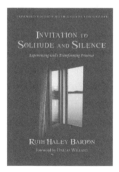

Invitation to Solitude and Silence

ISBN 978-0-8308-3545-4

Invitation to Solitude and Silence *Audio Book*

available from www.oasisaudio.com

www.thetransformingcenter.org